KNOCKED DOWN, BUT NOT OUT

KNOCKED DOWN, BUT NOT OUT

BILLY JOE DAUGHERTY

Destiny Image₍ᵣ₎ Publishers, Inc.
P.O. Box 310
Shippensburg, PA 17257-0310

*"Speaking to the Purposes of God for This Generation
and for the Generations to Come"*

This book and all other Destiny Image, Revival Press, MercyPlace, Fresh Bread, Destiny Image Fiction, and Treasure House books are available at Christian bookstores and distributors worldwide.

For a U.S. bookstore nearest you, call
1-800-722-6774.

For more information on foreign distributors, call
717-532-3040.

Or reach us on the Internet:
www.destinyimage.com

ISBN 10: 0-7684-2391-0

ISBN 13: 978-0-7684-2391-4

For Worldwide Distribution, Printed in the U.S.A.

3 4 5 6 7 8 9 10 11 / 09 08 07 06

CONTENTS

INTRODUCTION

O<small>N</small> Sunday, November 20, 2005, during the 11 a.m. service altar call, as I was praying with individuals prior to praying corporately for those at the altar as well as those in the congregation, a man at the altar punched me in my left eye, nearly knocking me over.

I returned to the platform, but while this man was being escorted out of the service, he hit another one of our ministers. It's called "a parting shot!" Then he hit a security officer, which is why he landed in jail and was ultimately returned to the mental institution where he had been treated previously.

My message that morning was on giving thanks and praise to God continually, no matter what happens. With that clearly in my mind after the punch, I led the congregation in praise and thanksgiving to the Lord for His grace and mercy not for the incident that happened, but in the midst of it!

At that time, I remembered what Chancellor Oral Roberts had taught my wife, Sharon, and I when we were students at Oral Roberts University. "Don't strike back!" That is what God had told him years ago and I'd heard it many times since then. About 30 years ago, Roy Hicks also shared with me, "If you don't get bitter, you'll make it." So praising God in the midst of this incident was a truth that was very important to me.

Sharon and I have been in a lot of situations through the years when unexpected things have happened in the congregation or crowd. Whether it was while preaching in Sierra Leone, Haiti, Peru, Pakistan, India, Norway, or most recently in Russia in the Ural Mountain region, regardless of the situation—including this fresh assault—we forgive people and then we go right on with what God assigned us to do.

As a congregation and for me personally, we prayed for the man who had slugged me and we asked the Holy Spirit to do a work in his life.

My eye was swollen, but thank God, there was no damage to my vision. I am very grateful to Dr. Scott Cordray who took me across the street to CityPlex after the service. I ended up with two stitches in the area where I had been cut. Dr. Douglas Holte, a physician in attendance, also examined me. Thank God for doctors!

During the week that followed, while Sharon and I were at the airport, a woman we didn't know came up to us and made a comment about what had happened during Sunday's service. She had seen the incident replayed on TV and in our conversation this lady said something to me that touched my heart. She was going through a divorce.

Suddenly, it hit me: Sometimes we're bleeding on the outside, and sometimes there is bleeding on the inside. Mine was on the outside that day—people could see it. But for many people who have been hit with something bad, there is brokenness in their hearts, pain in their thoughts, and hurting in their emotions—nobody can see that they are bleeding on the inside.

God gave me a message about what to do when life gives you a hit and you are hurt and wounded. Perhaps there has been abuse, a violation, a broken home, abandonment, rejection, loss of a job, loss of income, a demotion, a legal entanglement, a negative medical diagnosis, or pain in the physical body from an illness in your life. When there is pain and hurt, what do you do?

We believe in a God of miracles, a God who delivers, a God who saves, and a God who heals and restores. That's my prayer for you, that you will be saved, healed, delivered, and restored.

The video of the "punch" was aired on multiple local, national, and international television stations and networks, and on the Internet all over the world. Because of the massive response from people who viewed it, throughout this book, we will look at some Word-based principles that you can apply when you're in a tight spot or when you've been hit unexpectedly. These truths will help you overcome and move on through to total victory!

You can weather the storms of life, turn your scars into stars, and literally start over after failure or defeat, as you make room for repentance and surrender yourself totally to the lordship of Jesus Christ.

It's time to celebrate Jesus as you get back up and praise on through once you've been knocked down. In the Amplified Bible, First Corinthians 15:57 contains a beautiful promise for you: "Thanks be to God, Who gives us the victory [making us conquerors] through our Lord Jesus Christ." You can be assured that God will help you get back up so you can continue your destiny, moving forward in Him!

—Billy Joe Daugherty

And whenever you stand praying, if you have anything against anyone, forgive him, that your Father in heaven may also forgive you your trespasses. But if you do not forgive, neither will your Father in heaven forgive your trespasses.

Mark 11:25-26

Chapter 1

WHAT IS YOUR RESPONSE WHEN THE SQUEEZE IS ON?

W HEN you're in a tight spot, your response exposes the real you. Jesus said, *"Out of the abundance of the heart the mouth speaks"* (Matt. 12:34). And, Proverbs 4:23 says, *"Keep your heart with all diligence, for out of it spring the issues of life."*

The squeeze was on me, so to speak, when I was punched in the eye at an altar call at the conclusion of a service in the Mabee Center on the Oral Roberts University Campus. I was nearly knocked down, but I wasn't knocked out! I did exactly what I had just preached about. I praised my way through and the service concluded in an orderly, Holy Spirit anointed manner!

With blood trickling down the left side of my face, I continued the service and said, "Let's give thanks and praise to the Lord Jesus." As far as I know, it was the first time this man attended a service at Victory Christian Center. Obviously, he had some unresolved issues in his life.

When bad or unexpected things happen, you need to forgive people and pray for the blessing of the Lord to come upon them. As a congregation, we thanked God for the blessing of the Lord upon this man's life, and we asked Him to pour His Spirit out upon him. We thanked God for His grace and mercy in the situation.

Sometimes we see an offense or an assault coming our way, and sometimes we don't. I didn't see this one coming!

HOW TO RESPOND TO AN ASSAILANT

In Matthew 5:44 Jesus said, *"Love your enemies, bless those who curse you, do good to those who hate you, and pray for those who spitefully use you and persecute you."* When we respond to offenses and altercations in this manner, the Spirit of God will work. I am believing that this man will be transformed, and I am grateful that he came to the house of the Lord. I forgive him, and our entire congregation forgave him, knowing that he didn't really understand what he did.

Tulsa Mayor Bill LaFortune was in attendance at this service, and he and his wife, Cathy, came to the platform to hug me, as he said, "for everyone present." Then, in response to the message I had just preached and the incident that had just happened, he said, "Praise on through everything, every opposition that comes at you. We love you so much. Hang in there and praise on through."

A lifestyle of praise and thanksgiving is one of the primary ways to become more than a conqueror in this life, regardless of the hits or offenses that come your way!

If you abide in My word, you are My disciples indeed. And you shall know the truth, and the truth shall make you free.

John 8:31-32

Arise, shine; for your light has come! And the glory of the Lord is risen upon you.

Isaiah 60:1

Chapter 2

THREE BIBLE EXAMPLES
OF BEING HIT

REMEMBER, it's up to you to respond with praise and thanksgiving when you are hit. Other people have been hit and they came through their troubles victorious. One of the best places to look for others who were hit with unexpected troubles is in the Bible. Learning about their response to the hit will help us deal with what we are facing. Let's look briefly at the lives of Paul and Silas, Joseph, and Daniel.

PAUL AND SILAS

One of the greatest stories in the Bible of people who were hit and who praised their way on through to victory is Paul and Silas.

In Acts 16, Paul cast the devil out of a young woman who had a fortune-telling spirit (a spirit of divination). The men who owned her used her to tell people's fortunes for payment. When Paul cast the devil out of her, the money dried up for those men because she couldn't tell anyone's fortune anymore. The men were so angry that they reported the incident to the city authorities. The authorities didn't check to see if Paul was a Roman citizen, for it was against the law to beat and jail a Roman citizen without a fair hearing and trial. Paul was a Roman citizen but the officials beat Paul and Silas, put them in the inner part of the prison, and fastened their hands and feet in chains and stocks.

Now, think about this picture. Paul had been illegally mistreated because of prejudice. He was judged by his appearance and deemed not worthy of being a Roman citizen. Officials didn't even ask.

Paul and Silas were in pain and locked in stocks. No one had the power in the natural to get them out of jail or to plead their case. But they knew someone who could intervene for them!

Acts 16:25 says, *"But at midnight...."* This may be your midnight hour, your darkest moment. You say, "Pastor, I can do this on Sunday, but you don't know what I'm going through." In spite of the pain, injustice, mistreatment, and conditions, *"At midnight Paul and Silas were praying and singing hymns to God, and the prisoners were listening to them."*

Sometimes people say, "Well, I've got praise in my heart." It's so deep down in there, no one has ever heard it or seen it! The prisoners heard Paul and Silas praying and singing praises to God.

Suddenly there was a great earthquake [when you start praising God, things are going to be shaken up], so that the foundations of the prison were shaken; and immediately all the doors were opened and everyone's chains were loosed. And the keeper of the prison, awaking from sleep and seeing the prison doors open, supposing the prisoners had fled, drew his sword and was about to kill himself. But Paul called with a loud voice, saying, 'Do yourself no harm, for we are all here.' Then he called for a light, ran in, and fell down trembling before Paul and Silas. And he brought them out and said, "Sirs, what must I do to be saved?"

Then they spoke the word of the Lord to him and to all who were in his house.

And he took them the same hour of the night and washed their stripes. And immediately he

and all his family were baptized (Acts
16:26-33).

Your praise can turn disaster into revival! You
can turn your situations around today right where
you are. If you haven't got money to pay your bills,
remember what I said. Take care of business and get
a job. Not only get a job but also, be there on time.
Not only be there on time, but also do the work in an
excellent manner. Not only work in excellence, but
also do it with a good attitude. While you are there,
go ahead and praise God. God is going to make a
way for you, just as He did for Paul and Silas.

JOSEPH

We find the story of Joseph in Genesis, chapters
37-50. Joseph had a dream at the age of 17 that he
would one day be a world ruler. He shared that
dream with his family and his brothers became jealous. They wanted to kill him, but instead, they sold
him to a band of traders who were headed to Egypt.
Then Joseph was sold to a man by the name of
Potiphar. Joseph worked for him and he was so successful and anointed that the man put Joseph in
charge of everything he owned.

One day Joseph was approached by Potiphar's
wife who tried to seduce him. Facing the temptation,

he did the best thing he could do. He ran. He did the right thing. Potiphar's wife then accused him, slandered him, and as a result of being accused of attacking her, Joseph was thrown in prison unjustly. This account is found in Genesis 39:

> *But the Lord was with Joseph and showed him mercy, and He gave him favor in the sight of the keeper of the prison. And the keeper of the prison committed to Joseph's hand all the prisoners who were in the prison; whatever they did there, it was his doing. The keeper of the prison did not look into anything that was under Joseph's authority, because the Lord was with him; and whatever he did, the Lord made it prosper* (Genesis 39:21-23).

Imagine you are a young teenage boy, your whole family rejects you, you are sold as a slave into a foreign land, and now you're in prison where no one knows you or cares about you. Joseph didn't complain and sulk; he applied himself and worked hard so that eventually the jailer put him in charge of the entire prison.

There's an important point that needs to be stressed here: If you will trust God's anointing, no matter how far someone tries to put you down, you are going to pop right back up to the top!

Joseph didn't get into bitterness toward his brothers or toward Potiphar's wife. Two of Pharaoh's servants were also placed in prison—a butler and a baker. Both the butler and the baker had dreams and Joseph had the supernatural gift from God to interpret those dreams. The butler was restored to his position with Pharaoh just as Joseph said. The Pharaoh hung the baker just as Joseph had interpreted (Gen. 40:13, 22).

Joseph said to the butler, *"Remember me when it is well with you, and please show kindness to me; make mention of me to Pharaoh, and get me out of this house"* (Gen. 40:14). Once the butler was released, he forgot about Joseph.

Not only was Joseph sold by his brothers, slandered by a woman, and illegally placed in jail, now he was forgotten in the prison.

Joseph got hit again and again. He was getting hit in unexpected ways. Bad things happened that he had not planned. Even though Joseph had a series of bad things happen to him, he just kept on serving.

Two years after the butler was restored to his position, Pharaoh had a dream and no one could interpret it. The butler said, "I did time with a guy in prison who can interpret dreams." Joseph was called to interpret Pharaoh's dream.

> *Pharaoh said to Joseph, "I have had a dream, and there is no one who can interpret it. But I have heard it said of you that you can understand a dream, to interpret it." So Joseph answered Pharaoh, saying, "It is not in me; God will give Pharaoh an answer of peace"* (Genesis 41:15-16).

Pharaoh shared his dreams with Joseph and Joseph interpreted them, saying, *"The dreams are one"* (v. 26). The interpretation was that there would be seven years of great plenty, followed by seven years of famine. Then, by the wisdom of God, Joseph gave a detailed strategy of how to prepare for the lean years that were coming.

The result: Pharaoh basically said, "Joseph, you're the man to carry out this plan!" In one day, Joseph went from prisoner to prime minister of the greatest nation on the face of the earth at that time.

How did this happen? Joseph had a dream and he wouldn't let go of it. He chose to forgive and he didn't get bitter. He chose to apply himself and work rather than be angry and depressed.

The world is filled with a lot of people in the workplace whose performance is far below what it should be because they are discouraged, depressed, and angry. They are mad at the world so they are just going through the motions of working.

If you will get that stuff off of your back by forgiving, you can rise to the top, even if you're at the bottom of the prison! God has a way to bring you through to victory!

DANIEL

It is good to remember that other people have gone through bad hits, even though they were doing good things. Daniel helped the kings of Babylon and also the head of the Medes and Persian Empire that overthrew the Babylonian Empire. One after another, Daniel helped the kings. He had the wisdom of God and he was called to be a governor, one of the leaders. In fact, King Darius thought to put Daniel over the whole of the Empire (see Daniel 6).

When this word got out the other rulers, jealous of Daniel, decided, "We've got to get rid of Daniel." The only way they knew to do it was to challenge his commitment to God.

Daniel 6:3-5 says:

Then this Daniel distinguished himself above the governors and satraps, because an excellent spirit was in him; and the king gave thought to setting him over the whole realm. So the governors and satraps sought to find some charge against Daniel concerning the kingdom; but they could find no charge or fault, because he was faithful; nor was there any error or fault found in him. Then these men said, "We shall not find any charge against this Daniel unless we find it against him concerning the law of his God."

These men went to King Darius and requested that he make a decree, stating, "...Whoever petitions any god or man for thirty days, except you, O king, shall be cast into the den of lions." (Dan. 6:7).

King Darius established the decree and because he was on an ego trip, he signed it, not knowing that one of his best men was about to be caught by it. He would soon discover that Daniel was not a man-pleaser; he was a God-pleaser.

When word got out that you couldn't pray to anyone except the king, Daniel prayed just as he had always done. Daniel 6:10 says,

Now when Daniel knew that the writing was signed, he went home. And in his upper room, with his windows open toward Jerusalem, he knelt down on his knees three times that day, and prayed and gave thanks before his God, as was his custom since early days.

Many people would shut their mouths out of fear of losing their job, their pension, or a promotion. But Daniel didn't compromise his relationship with God because he knew that promotion comes from God.

Daniel prayed in public just like he had always done and the other governors knew it. They were waiting to catch him, because they knew he did it. Daniel threw open the window in his house and they could hear him praying. They took it to the king, and sadly, the king had to keep his decree because the law of the Medes and Persians could not be reversed.

As a result, Daniel was sentenced to death in the lions' den. That was a bad day when a man came to Daniel's door and said, "You are going to die. You will be thrown to the lions." This is a perfect example of bad things happening to good people. This situation was something unexpected that Daniel hadn't planned on, yet it happened. The night Daniel spent in the lions' den, God shut the mouths of the lions. God stood up for Daniel as Daniel stood up for the Lord.

There may be some people who want to devour you, but God is going to shut their mouths. Daniel 6:26 contains a very interesting public announcement:

I [King Darius] *make a decree that in every dominion of my kingdom men must tremble and fear before the God of Daniel. For He is the living God, and steadfast forever; His kingdom is the one which shall not be destroyed, and His dominion shall endure to the end.*

Just imagine this in a kingdom that worshiped the king, idols, and the golden statue of Babylon. Now there's a public announcement that spreads across all the provinces that the God of Daniel, Jehovah, is the living God!

God will turn your circumstances around, just as he did for Paul and Silas, Joseph, and Daniel.

For exaltation comes neither from the east nor from the west nor from the south. But God is the Judge: He puts down one, and exalts another.

Psalm 75: 6-7

But thanks be to God, who gives us the victory through our Lord Jesus Christ.

1 Corinthians 15:57

Chapter 3

GOD WILL TURN YOUR SITUATIONS AROUND!

Let's look at Genesis 50:19-21 when the Lord used Joseph to speak a word to his brothers after his father's death.

After Joseph was placed in the position of prime minister of Egypt his brothers came to get food because of a severe famine in the land. They didn't know that Joseph was the prime minister. Joseph gave them food, and the day came when he revealed himself to them. Of course, they were in terror because of how they treated him. Then, when their father died, they were really afraid because they thought Joseph would kill them. Instead, Joseph spoke this word to them:

Do not be afraid, for am I in the place of God? But as for you, you meant evil against me; but God meant it for good, in order to bring it about as it is this day, to save many people alive. Now therefore, do not be afraid; I will provide for you and your little ones. And he comforted them and spoke kindly to them (Genesis 50:19-21).

God put Joseph in a place where he would be able to save many people. Salvation also came in the land of the Medes and the Persians because the king himself broadcast Daniel's testimony. God has a way of getting His message out. In the cases of Daniel, Joseph, and Paul and Silas, they were hit with something bad, but God turned it around for great good.

What the devil sends for disaster is going to turn into a Holy Ghost overflow! Get ready! This is your time for miracles, to believe that what God said, He will do.

GOD IS FOR YOU!

By an act of your own will, you can decide to let God turn your scars into stars from stumbling blocks to stepping-stones! He can turn the bad things that have happened to you into things that will work for your good.

Sometimes bad things happen because of our own mistakes, faults, or sins. Sometimes they happen because of the mistakes of others, their shortcomings, sins, and failures. Then, there are bad things that sometimes happen because we are doing something good. In such a case, it is an attack or an assault from the enemy to distract you from doing the will of God, but you can overcome it. Paul said, *"Yes, and all who desire to live godly in Christ Jesus will suffer persecution"* (2 Tim. 3:12).

If you set your sails to go against the enemy, you will encounter some opposition and persecution for living in a godly manner. Do not become discouraged! God has a word for you, *"Fear not, for I am with you; be not dismayed, for I am your God. I will strengthen you, yes, I will help you, I will uphold you with My righteous right hand"* (Isa. 41:10).

In the life of Jesus as well as in the life of Paul, people didn't exactly stand up and cheer because they were healing the sick and casting out devils. While some people were happy, others were greatly disturbed by these miracles.

Stephen was stoned to death, and James was beheaded. Paul was persecuted constantly, not for doing wrong, but for doing right.

The good news for us is that Jesus said, *"In the world you will have tribulation; but be of good cheer, I have overcome the world"* (John 16:33). Because Jesus has already overcome the world, we need to see ourselves from His perspective seated in heavenly places with Him! (See Ephesians 2:6.)

GOD WILL HELP YOU!

Not only should you remember that bad things have happened to others and that God is for you, remember, God is going to help you!

In John 10:10 in the *Amplified Bible* Jesus said, *"I came that* [you] *may have and enjoy life, and have it in abundance (to the full, till it overflows)."* God is our Helper, our strength, the One who will lift us up.

Romans 8:31 says, *"If God is for us, who can be against us?"* Think of this. If God is for you, who can prevail against you? Joseph's brothers were against him, but they didn't prevail over him. Daniel had all the governors and leaders against him, but they didn't prevail over him. Paul and Silas had officials who were in positions of authority come against them, but they didn't prevail over them. It is important that we get this word inside of us: *If God is for us, no one can prevail against us!*

Romans 8:28 says, *"And we know that all things work together for good to those who love God, to those who are the called according to His purpose."* Are you called according to His purpose? Then you qualify to say, *all things are working together for good in my life!*

Praise is a reflection of you *believing* these truths. A lot of people say, "Well, I don't know what's going to happen." You do! All things are going to work together for good in your life!

REPENTANCE AND FORGIVENESS: KEYS TO YOUR TURNAROUND

If you have failed and sinned, repent. God will not force anyone to repent. Sometimes bad things happen because people have done wrong things. If you have done some bad things, there is good news. Your sins can be forgiven. God says, *"Their sins and their lawless deeds I will remember no more"* (Heb. 10:17). Romans 4:7 says, *"Blessed are those whose lawless deeds are forgiven, and whose sins are covered."*

If someone has hurt you, then *you must choose to forgive* that person! Forgiveness is not a feeling and it is not an emotion. It is a decision. Always remember, forgiveness is a choice. It is based on what God did for you when He forgave you through Jesus' death on the cross.

Ephesians 4:32 says it this way: *"And be kind to one another, tenderhearted, forgiving one another, even as God in Christ forgave you."* I need forgiveness so I am going to be a forgiver. I need mercy so I am going to show mercy.

How much forgiveness do you need? Put it in proper perspective. In the Lord's Prayer, Jesus taught that we are to forgive others, even as our Father has forgiven us our trespasses; if we don't forgive others, neither will our Father in heaven forgive us (Matt. 6:12,14,15).

If you make a decision to forgive, forget, and release your assailants and offenders, the blessing of God cannot be stopped from coming upon your life. The very things that are scars will be turned into stars! The very things that hurt you can become the key to your promotion or the platform from which you go to the next level of success. They will serve as stepping-stones for you.

If you nurse and rehearse your scars and curse your offenders, your scars will become like a millstone around your neck and that will be the end of a fruitful life for you.

You may be thinking that everywhere Joseph went he had a battle. That's true, but God always delivered him. David, who was delivered by God from many troubles, wrote in Psalm 34:19, *"Many are the afflictions of the righteous, but the Lord delivers him out of them all."*

It was the same in Paul's life. He could have quit after that first experience in the Philippian jail. He cast the devil out of a girl, and the next thing he knew, he was in jail for it. He could have said, "Lord, if this is what I get for preaching, then that's it. If that is Your reward, forget it!"

Instead, Paul chose to forgive, forget, and release, and at midnight he led a celebration of praise to God. As a result, God opened the prison doors and a jailhouse revival broke out!

Think of it! What was a stumbling block and a scar to Paul became a testimony that has literally catapulted millions of people into victory!

Your trial or your most horrible experience can become a terrific testimony, depending on your response!

I'm sure you've heard the old saying, "Your attitude will determine your altitude." It's not the things that happen to you or how fast the wind comes against you that count toward success. *It's your response that counts.* It's the way you set your wings, because the stronger the winds, the higher you will soar!

JESUS IS OUR EXAMPLE: "FATHER, FORGIVE THEM."

In Luke 23:34, with spikes in His hands and feet, a crown of thorns on His head, and a back that had been beaten with the Roman scourge, Jesus said, *"Father, forgive them, for they do not know what they do."* It wasn't about an emotional feeling. It was about a decision based on the love of God. If you have Christ in your life, then you can do what Jesus did.

Jesus is the ultimate forgiver. He is the ultimate example of rising up after He got knocked down. He is the ultimate example of going ahead and praising and giving thanks. We need to make a decision we are going to follow Jesus' example.

When I was punched in the eye during a church altar call, I came back on stage and we, as a congregation, chose to forgive the man. We prayed for the Lord to bless him and do a work in his life to transform him. Then we all began to praise God while the blood was flowing from my eye down my face.

WE PRAISED OUR WAY THROUGH A FIRE THAT DESTROYED OUR HOME

I remember the night our house burned down in 1991 between 1:00 and 2:00 in the morning. The house was totally destroyed, so much so that after the fire it had to be bulldozed. That night we got everyone out except two of our children, Ruthie and Paul. I had to go back in to get them. First, I got Ruthie out, and then I went back in again and got Paul.

Once we were all out, we gathered on the front porch of our neighbor's home, the Browns, and we watched our house burn. Fire trucks were everywhere. Together, we praised God and worshiped Him with all of us holding on to each other. The things we owned were being burned, but we still had our lives and our relationship with God.

Here is a very important point. Many people spend all of their lives asking, "Why?" They never give one thought to thanking and praising God that they are still alive. If you will praise God and not focus on problems, God will take you right on through from glory to glory. We purchased another home and furniture. Our youth director at that time, Ray Barnard, who is now a pastor in Philadelphia said, "Pastor, your old clothes *needed* to burn!"

Today we have better than what we ever had before. A month after the fire in 1991, we began the crusades in Russia, and continued them for 18 months in a row. Thousands upon thousands of people were born again. We know it was the devil's attack to try to stop the harvest that was about to come in Russia. We were there when the wall of Communism came down.

In 1980 God had spoken to us, "There will be giant harvesting machines that will go across Russia and people will reap the end-time harvest of souls in that nation." Then God spoke, "You will be one of them." Even though there was an attempt to stop that from happening, we decided to praise God on through!

Years ago Sharon wrote a song, "Turn It Around," that Richard Roberts used as his theme song when he started his daily television program that I co-hosted with him for three or four years. God will turn your situation around as you praise on through! The song says that God will turn around your situation if you believe Him and choose to praise His name.

PRAISE STOPS THE ENEMY IN HIS TRACKS

In Psalm 8:2 David said, *"Out of the mouth of babes and nursing infants You have ordained strength, because of Your enemies, that You may silence the enemy and the avenger."* Jesus repeated this verse in Matthew 21:16. Jesus had just overturned the tables of the moneychangers because they had made the temple, called to be a house of prayer, *"a den of thieves"* (Matt. 21:13).

Little children were saying, *"Hosanna to the Son of David!"* (v. 15), and the religious leaders said, *"Do You hear what these are saying?"* (v. 16). In other words, "You need to stop these kids from saying that." Then Jesus said to them, "Have you never read, *'Out of the mouth of babes and nursing infants You have perfected praise'?"* (v. 16). Praise will cause strength to be released and it will stop the enemy in his tracks.

Perhaps you are saying, "I don't know what good it does to praise God." I can tell you that praise will stop the devil—the avenger and your attacker. It brings glory and honor to God and sends confusion into the camp of the enemy.

Praise is the ultimate form of faith. When the circumstances are wrong, people are saying things, and you've got all types of feelings and emotions going on, keep on praising Him. Praising Him *in the midst* is evidence you believe the Word of God rather than the circumstances or your feelings. In time, we will be praising God for all eternity.

In Mark 11:24 Jesus said, *"Whatever things you ask when you pray, believe that you receive them, and you will have them."* In Matthew 9:29 Jesus said, *"According to your faith let it be to you."* If you pray and believe you receive something, then you are going to go ahead and praise God at that moment, before you ever see the manifestation of your answer.

GET UP AND KEEP ON GOING!

When you get hit in an unexpected way, you have to get up and keep on going. It's not the time to quit. It's not the time to fall into depression. It's not the time to get distracted with anger. Keep on doing what God has assigned you to do. Just stay with it!

When I was punched unexpectedly at the end of the service, some people said, "You just went on with the service." Of course I did. We were in the middle of an altar call. It doesn't matter if you are bleeding or you are hit, people need to be saved. That day I was teaching on praising God and praising on through. We need to do it, forgive, and keep on going regardless of natural circumstances.

Daniel kept on doing what he was told to do and he kept on praying. Joseph kept on serving faithfully. Paul and Silas kept on praising. Keep on doing what you are supposed to be doing, no matter what. If you don't quit, you can't lose. You may get knocked down, but you are not knocked out or destroyed!

RIGHT RESPONSE WILL TURN THE HEARTS OF THE UNSAVED

When bad things happen and you have the right response, it sends a message that penetrates the hearts of the unsaved. That's part of what happened with me. People who may not have had an interest in the Lord saw the Lord work in this situation and they have responded.

Second Corinthians 4:3-11 says:

Even if our gospel is veiled, it is veiled to those who are perishing, whose minds the god of this age has blinded, who do not believe, lest the light of the gospel of the glory of Christ, who is the image of God, should shine on them.

For we do not preach ourselves, but Christ Jesus the Lord, and ourselves your bondservants for Jesus' sake.

For it is the God who commanded light to shine out of darkness, who has shone in our hearts to give the light of the knowledge of the glory of God in the face of Jesus Christ.

But we have this treasure in earthen vessels, that the excellence of the power may be of God and not of us. [In other words, if something good happens, everyone is going to know it had to be God. That's the point Paul was making.]

We are hard-pressed on every side, yet not crushed; we are perplexed, but not in despair [In other words, we may not have all the answers, but we are not giving up.];

Persecuted, but not forsaken; struck down, but not destroyed [Remember that the next time you get hit!]—

Always carrying about in the body the dying of the Lord Jesus, that the life of Jesus also may be manifested in our body [In other words, when bad things take place and we respond the right way, the life of Jesus is broadcast in the mortal body, the one we are in right now.]

For we who live are always delivered to death for Jesus' sake, that the life of Jesus also may be manifested in our mortal flesh.

Hard-pressed, but not crushed; perplexed, but not in despair; persecuted, but not forsaken; struck down, but not destroyed. Do you relate?

Paul was saying that when you face difficult circumstances, problems, and trials and you respond with the love of God, the light of the gospel is going to penetrate those who have been blinded, because of what they see in your life.

It's so important that we respond correctly, not just to get back up on top, but because someone is going to see our witness. They need to know there is a living God!

He also brought me up out of a horrible pit, out of the miry clay, and set my feet upon a rock, and established my steps.

Psalm 40:2

Him, being delivered by the determined purpose and foreknowledge of God, you have taken by lawless hands, have crucified, and put to death; whom God raised up, having loosed the pains of death, because it was not possible that He should be held by it.

Acts 2:23-24

Chapter 4

OVERCOMING YOUR HITS

AT some time in life, every person faces a hit or a storm in the form of situations, circumstances, obstacles, problems, and difficulties. These hits take you off the course God would have you run. They deter you and keep you from being all God wants you to be, from having all God wants you to have, and from doing all He wants you to do.

Sometimes the hits are from the devil. Sometimes problems reach you through other people's problems and you are affected because of your association with them. Sometimes you create your own storm or challenge by your own mistakes.

It is most important for you to know that *you are going to make it* and to know how to make it as an overcomer. The hits in life do not make you or break you. It is the Word of God working in your life that makes you victorious, and it is a lack of God's Word that makes people fail. The storm or difficulty merely reveals whether you are a doer of the Word or just a hearer of it.

JESUS FACED MANY HITS

If you are living for Jesus, you've taken a stand against the devil. This means you will encounter him head-on. Wherever Paul preached and ministered, he was opposed. Jesus, from His very first message, was criticized and ridiculed. In fact, in His first hometown sermon, they tried to throw Him off a cliff and kill Him. That was just the beginning of the opposition He encountered during his time of teaching and sharing. Everywhere He went, Jesus faced storms: criticism, slander, and wrong words spoken about Him. If Jesus overcame all these storms, you can overcome all of the hits you receive in life because He lives in you!

Sometimes the storm or hit that people face is sickness or disease that tries to rob them of physical health. Sometimes it is a financial hit. You add up the bills and they exceed the income. Then there's a storm of worry and anxiety that tries to come against you over a family situation.

Some people face storms related to a relationship, with difficulties and misunderstandings, when people say critical things. Thank God, you and I are going to get through these storms.

Jesus lives in you by faith. Believe He is in you now and expect Him to help you overcome every hit or storm through the faith He has given you.

STRATEGIES FOR OVERCOMING HITS

Here are nine strategies for overcoming the storms or hits that may come into your life:

1. Build Your House on the Rock.

Matthew 7:24-27 says:

Therefore whoever hears these sayings of Mine, and does them, I will liken him to a wise man who built his house on the rock: And the rain descended, the floods came, and the winds blew and beat on that house; and it did not fall for it was founded on the rock.

But everyone who hears these sayings of Mine, and does not do them, will be like a foolish man who built his house on the sand: And the rain descended, the floods came, and

*the winds blew and beat on that house; and it
fell. And great was its fall.*

The rains, winds, and floods came against both
houses. One was affected and the other wasn't.
Jesus said all of us would encounter storms (or unexpected hits). Those who hear and do the Word of
God will stand. Those who only hear but don't do the
Word will fall. Each one of us decides whether we
will stand or fall by what we do with God's Word.

2. Become a **Doer** of God's Word.

Another key for overcoming the hits in your life
is to become a doer of God's Word. The wise man
did the Word. Both the wise man and the foolish
man *heard* the Word, but the wise man became a
doer of it.

You'll be wise to become a doer of the Word that
you know—you already know enough to put you
over. If you simply do what you already know, you
can be victorious in every area of your life. I am saying that for a reason—many people improperly per-
ceive that the solution to their problems is gaining
more knowledge. In some cases, that may be true.
But for the people who have heard the Word over a
period of time, it is not necessarily *more* truth that
they need, but it's *applying* the truth they have
already received.

Jesus didn't say the man who stood was the man who got more information. In fact, He says they both had the information. The overcomer was the one who took what he knew, applied it to the situation, and put it into practice. He became a doer of the Word of God. In other words, there was a corresponding action.

Let's look at Luke 8:22-25:

Now it happened, on a certain day, that He got into a boat with His disciples. And He said to them, "Let us cross over to the other side of the lake." And they launched out.

But as they sailed He fell asleep. And a windstorm came down on the lake, and they were filling with water, and were in jeopardy.

And they came to Him and awoke Him, saying, "Master, Master, we are perishing!" Then He arose and rebuked the wind and the raging of the water. And they ceased, and there was a calm.

But He said to them, "Where is your faith?" And they were afraid, and marveled, saying to one another, "Who can this be? For He commands even the winds and water, and they obey Him!"

Jesus asked the disciples, "Where is your faith?" All the disciples could see were disaster, problems, and difficulties. Jesus didn't commend them for waking Him up! He stopped the storm, but in essence, it was a rebuke! He said, "Where is your faith?" Jesus was saying, "You already have the faith to stop the storm and get through it. Why didn't you use it? Where is your faith?"

Faith and fear repel each other. They are opposites. If fear rises up, faith goes out the door. If faith rises up, fear goes out the door. This is a key factor to coming through your storms (or hits): Become a doer of the Word by releasing your faith and dispelling the fear.

Fear paralyzes while faith activates. When you believe what God says and stand on it, fear will leave you. But when you believe the circumstances and words that the devil brings, faith will leave. First John 5:4 says, *"This is the victory that has overcome the world, our faith."* Choose to believe the Word and doubt the lies of the enemy.

James had something to say about becoming *doers* as well as *hearers* of the Word. In James 1:22 he says, *"But be doers of the word, and not hearers only, deceiving yourselves."* James rephrased the words of Jesus recorded in Matthew 7:24.

Someone who just hears the teaching of the Word, but doesn't apply it to their circumstances is self-deceived, because they think since they've heard the message it is going to work. But it doesn't work because you've heard it—it works because you apply it! It's like Windex Window Cleaner. It doesn't clean the window while in the bottle. You have to spray it on, and then you have to rub the window with it until the dirt is removed.

Just because you have God's Word inside of you doesn't mean it is going to do the work. *You* have to apply it to each situation. Don't just be a hearer. Be a doer of God's Word.

James 1:23-24 says:

> *For if anyone is a hearer of the word and not a doer, he is like a man observing his natural face in a mirror; For he observes himself, goes away, and immediately forgets what kind of man he was.*

He looks in the mirror of God's Word. The Bible is referred to as a mirror. It gives the image of God inside of us. When we look into the Word, we see who we really are in Him. We see the new creation God has made us to be in Christ Jesus.

Whoever looks into the Word and is just a hearer and not a doer, forgets who he really is. On Sunday in church, you may say, "I'm more than a conqueror." On Monday the storm comes. You had better look in the mirror again! Say it out loud: "I am more than a conqueror!"

3. Agree with God's Word.

When a hit comes, are you going to say what the hit or circumstance dictates or what the Word says?

Here is the real battle. Some people think, *If I say what the Word says, I'll be lying.* It all depends upon what you call truth. If you call the circumstances of the world a greater truth than God's Word, then in your own perspective, it would be lying. But if you get a revelation that God's Word is greater than all circumstances, His Word will remain when the whole world is burned up.

Look into the Word. Jesus said, *"Heaven and earth will pass away, but My words will by no means pass away"* (Matt. 24:35).

When you begin to understand the eternal truth of the Word, then you'll understand that when you are saying what the Word says, you are not lying. You will finally be telling the truth!

As long as you speak your feelings, that's the way it is going to be. But if you will speak God's Word in the face of any situation, it will lift you up to be what it says. You have to keep looking in the mirror of the Word. This is why Joshua 1:8 says,

This Book of the Law shall not depart from your mouth, but you shall meditate in it day and night, that you may observe to do according to all that is written in it. For then you will make your way prosperous, and then you will have good success.

Rise early each day and meditate on what the Word of God says about you: I have the mind of Christ. I have the wisdom of God. Christ dwells in me through the power of the Holy Spirit. As you speak the Word, the reality of it will begin to take place.

Some people have said, "Well, I said it three times and it didn't work. I confessed that all my needs would be met last week and the money didn't come. I'm giving up on that stuff!" There's more to it than just saying it for a little while. I'm talking about committing your heart to the Word of God and becoming locked into it.

Take the attitude, "If it doesn't work for anyone else in the entire world, it's going to work for me. I am not basing my faith on the Word's fulfillment in any other person's life." Some people say, "I know so-and-so or Grandma so-and-so. They were good Christians and they believed the Word, but it didn't work for them."

I am not their judge, so I can't say anything about those people. I wasn't there, I don't know the situation, but I do know this: *"God is not a man, that He should lie, nor a son of man, that He should repent. Has He said, and will He not do? Or has He spoken, and will He not make it good?"* (Num. 23:19).

We've got to get to the point where we say: The Word is true. It works, and it is working in me! We must work the Word and let it work in us.

4. Don't Be Critical of Others.

You can negate the power of God with your words. One of the things you have to watch in the hits and storms is keeping your tongue from speaking evil about someone else. If you get into judgment and criticism, you can become an attacker of others in your time of difficulty. It can rob you of your own faith. This is why Jesus spoke about forgiveness after speaking on mountain-moving faith:

> *And whenever you stand praying, if you have anything against anyone, forgive him, that your Father in heaven may also forgive you your trespasses. But if you do not forgive, neither will your Father in heaven forgive your trespasses* (Mark 11:25-26).

5. Hold Fast to the Confession of Your Faith.

Hebrews 10:23 KJV says, *"Let us hold fast the profession of our faith without wavering; (for he is faithful that promised)."* Hold fast to the confession or the words of your lips, without wavering, concerning what God has spoken to you. *Wavering* means to go back and forth.

Just because you don't understand something doesn't mean you can't believe in God or that His Word isn't working. We all don't understand how a little seed put into the ground pops through the earth, but farmers believe it because they have seen it year after year. It's the same way with God's Word. Hold fast to your planting of the Word (the seed), for it *will* produce a harvest of like kind to what you are speaking.

Therefore do not cast away your confidence, which has great reward. For you have need of endurance [the King James Version says "patience"], *so that after you have done the will of God, you may receive the promise* (Hebrews 10:35-36).

6. Release Your Faith.

The three primary ways of releasing your faith are: Believing the Word, Speaking the Word, and Acting on the Word.

Believing the Word. You release your faith by what you believe in your heart.

Romans 10:17 says, *"So then faith comes by hearing, and hearing by the word of God."* When you hear the Word of the Lord and you believe it, faith rises up. *"Faith is the substance of things hoped for, the evidence of things not seen"* (Heb. 11:1). Faith is the *title deed* that you hold concerning those things that are unseen. You know you have them, because God's Word promises them to you.

Speaking the Word. You release your faith by the words you speak.

Second Corinthians 4:13 describes the spirit of faith: *"And since we have the same spirit of faith, according to what is written, I believed and therefore I spoke, we also believe and therefore speak."* The spirit of faith means that you are *believing and speaking* the Word according to what God has spoken.

To get through the hits you have received, you need to train your tongue to speak the right things consistently. It is difficult to lasso your tongue and wrestle it under control if you wait until you've been hit. When they are hit, many people run their mouth

90 miles an hour with doubt and unbelief. They repeat everything the doctors have said as if it came straight from God. They pronounce everything the world has said as if it is an edict from Jesus Himself.

Isaiah said, *"Who has believed our report?"* (Isa. 53:1). You must discipline your tongue to speak God's report. Proverbs 18:21 says, *"Death and life are in the power of the tongue...."* Proverbs 6:2 says, *"You are snared by the words of your mouth; you are taken by the words of your mouth."*

Jesus said, *"...For out of the abundance of the heart the mouth speaks"* (Matt.12:34). Get a hold on your tongue now! Make a decision that you are going to speak what God's Word says, regardless of what circumstances seem to dictate.

Jesus said to Peter, *"Indeed, Satan has asked for you, that he may sift you as wheat"* (Luke 22:31). I believe it's a revelation for every believer that satan wants to sift you and find out what's really inside of you. According to Matthew 7, the hits (or storms) are going to come against everyone. Through the storms and the hits, satan will try to sift you. What is deep down on the inside of you will surface when you are hit.

We have people in our ministry and some of our church members who have gone through terrible financial storms. We have had an opportunity to pray with many of them about their situation. In one instance, the man said over and over, "I'm going to make it. I'm going to make it." It looked like the whole world was going to crash in. Problem after problem came, but he said, "I'm going to make it." He did!

When the storm is raging or an unexpected hit comes, pick your nose up out of the water and breathe! Just hang on to what God has said and declare it out loud. Everything within your feeling realm may want to say what it looks like, but *faith* refuses to bow its knee to the system of this world. Faith won't compromise. It just keeps speaking what God's Word says.

Psalm 112:7-8 says that the person whose heart is fixed (steadfast) will not be moved when evil tidings come: *"He will not be afraid of evil tidings; his heart is steadfast, trusting in the Lord. His heart is established; he will not be afraid...."*

When the evil report comes, or when you are hit unexpectedly in any realm of life, if your heart is settled on God's Word, you can say, "My God is able. It is well with my soul."

Acting On the Word. The third part of releasing your faith is acting upon what God says. There is a corresponding action to everything you speak. You have to act like the Word is true.

How should the disciples have acted in the midst of a hit or a storm? They should have awakened

Jesus and said, "Jesus, we're going to stop this storm. Do You want to watch us?"

They could have stood up in the boat and acted on what they believed.

As you begin to act on what you believe, God will give you specific direction for the corresponding action. It may not always be the same thing. It is Spirit-directed faith.

The Israelites had to listen for God's direction in every battle they faced. In taking Jericho, they had to march around the city once a day for six days and seven times on the seventh day (Josh. 6:1-5). That was their act of faith. But in the next city, the action of faith was different.

7. Don't Let an Unexpected Hit Dictate Your Life.

Romans 8:35-37 says:

Who shall separate us from the love of Christ? Shall tribulation, or distress, or persecution, or famine, or nakedness, or peril, or sword?

As it is written: "For Your sake we are killed all day long; we are accounted as sheep for the slaughter." Yet in all these things we are more than conquerors through Him who loved us.

Paul was declaring that in any circumstance, you have the power to overcome. He also said:

> *I know how to be abased, and I know how to abound. Everywhere and in all things I have learned both to be full and to be hungry, both to abound and to suffer need.*
>
> *I can do all things through Christ who strengthens me* (Phil. 4:12-13).

In other words, Paul was saying, "Circumstances don't dictate my life. What dominates me is what God has done in me and what He is yet doing for me."

To get through your hits, you need to know who you are in Christ, through what Jesus has done for you at Calvary, in the resurrection and in the sending of the Holy Spirit, and to know what He's doing right now at the right hand of the Father. Hebrews 7:25 says that Jesus is making daily intercession for you and me.

You may ask for prayer from other people, which is important. But there is One you can count on who is continually praying *for* you—Jesus. He ever lives to make intercession for you. He is praying for you, not against you! He is praying for you to win!

Believe you are going to get through the hit you took. Expect God to help you. He cares about your life.

What God did for the apostle Paul, He will do for you. Declare out loud: "I am more than a conqueror through Him who loves me. I can do all things through Christ who strengthens me."

8. Count It All Joy!

I think James had terrific insight about coming through battles, hits, and storms. He said, *"My brethren, count it all joy when you fall into various trials"* (James 1:2).

What do you think this means? It means, "Get joyful when you encounter various trials, difficulties, and temptations." If you read this with natural eyes rather than with spiritual eyes, you will really miss the point. Nehemiah 8:10 says, *"For the joy of the Lord is your strength."*

What happens when you lose your joy? You lose your strength. Without strength, you can't overcome adversity. So what did James say? When you encounter a hit or a storm, start rejoicing, not *for* the hit or storm, but rejoice that *God is with you* and He is helping you.

Paul said, *"Rejoice in the Lord always. Again I will say, rejoice!"* (Phil. 4:4). He wrote this word from prison! Imagine someone in chains encouraging others to rejoice. Paul had learned the secret of victory and joy. Faith is joyful, so rejoice!

9. Leave the Past Behind.

Isaiah 43:18-19 says:

Do not remember the former things, nor consider the things of old.

Behold, I will do a new thing, now it shall spring forth; shall you not know it? I will even make a road in the wilderness and rivers in the desert.

To get through your hits, you have to forget about your past experiences and let go of those things that are behind you.

We can learn a lot from Joseph who took some very important steps to move forward when faced with hits. What has happened in your past is past, but what you *do* about the past will control your future. You may not have had control over what happened in the past, but you *do* have control over what will happen in your future. Your response to past situations will determine what will happen in your future.

As a baseball player in the position of shortstop, let's assume you miss a ground ball and you miss the throw to first base. The worst thing you can do next is kick the ground and worry about your errors. Why? Because there's another ball coming! If your mind is on the last mistake, you will never be able to handle the next situation. You'll commit the same error again.

This happened in a College World Series. An outstanding third baseman who had the lowest error percentage of all the third basemen in the nation committed three errors in a row. They had to pull him from the game because he got his mind on the errors and he kept making the same mistake over and over.

We can't always explain why something happens, but one thing we can do is ask for the grace of God to forget about it and leave it with God. There are other relatives, other situations, other circumstances, and other battles that you are going to have to face, and you need all of your energy focused on them rather than dwelling on your past.

If there is something the Lord has told you to do, but it has been delayed, today is the day to receive God's grace and begin again.

Perhaps there are things God has called you to do that you have either forgotten or deliberately said "no" to. You might be a Jonah. God told you to go to

Nineveh, and there you are sailing on a Mediterranean cruise, but you are about to hit a storm! Like Jonah, God has to get your attention and you're saying, "Lord, I'll pay my vows. I'll obey You."

Demonic spirits are sent to stop people in their calling. You must say "No!" to them. Faith in God breaks the power of the devil. The spoken Word drives out demonic power.

What are you to do when you run into the devil's yoke of bondage and oppression, his diversion or roadblocks? Just keep on running. Back up and run at it again with the Word of God coming out of your mouth!

In Philippians 3:13-14 Paul said:

Brethren, I do not count myself to have apprehended; but one thing I do, forgetting those things which are behind and reaching forward to those things which are ahead,

I press toward the goal for the prize of the upward call of God in Christ Jesus.

The prize of the high calling of God is in Christ Jesus. He is the prize. He is the trophy. He is the wreath. He is the goal. He is the purpose of your life, for in Him is life. In John 11:25 Jesus said, *"I am the resurrection and the life...."*

When the apostle Paul said, *"I do not count myself to have apprehended,"* he was saying, "I haven't arrived yet. I'm not perfect." But he continued, *"But one thing I do, forgetting those things which are behind...."*

Are there things in your past that you would like to forget? It takes God's grace to forget. Grace is God's power, ability, and enablement. It is not by your works but it is by His gift of grace that you are able to let go of the past knowing that because of Jesus' shed blood those things are wiped out as you accept His completed work at Calvary.

Today is a great day to forget and lay aside those things that are behind that are keeping you from going forward. If you are holding on to things of the past, it is impossible to reach out and receive the fresh and new. Paul said, "I let go of those things." Paul had some difficult years, yet as he wrote this, he had some great things to rejoice about.

Your future is going to be better than your past. You have everything to look forward to, because your future is out of this world!

If you can believe, all things are possible to him who believes.

Mark 9:23

Do not rejoice over me, my enemy; when I fall, I will arise; when I sit in darkness, the Lord will be a light to me.

Micah 7:8

For God has not given us a spirit of fear, but of power and of love and of a sound mind.

2 Timothy 1:7

Chapter 5

THERE'S STILL HOPE EVEN IF YOU'RE DOWN FOR THE COUNT

Yes, there's hope for you! You can start over. God put the principle of a new start in the entire universe. In Genesis 1, He worked six days, and on the seventh day He rested. Sunday starts a new week all over again. We give praise to God as we celebrate on Sundays, because it is resurrection day. Jesus arose on this day, and the early Church began to worship on the first day of the week.

We celebrate a new day every day because the earth rotates every 24 hours. No matter how dark it gets in the night, morning always comes. A new moon comes up monthly. Every year we have a new beginning as the earth makes one complete revolution around the sun during that one-year period. Then it starts all over again.

After winter comes spring. God said, *"While the earth remains, seedtime and harvest, cold and heat, winter and summer, and day and night shall not cease"* (Gen. 8:22).

God put the principle of starting over in the earth. If you have a bad crop one year, you can start over and plant a new crop the next year! Each year brings a new harvest.

The Bible is filled with accounts of people beginning again. God made a beautiful, perfect Garden and put Adam and Eve in it. In spite of its perfection, they fell. The moment they fell, God initiated a new beginning. He said the seed of woman would bruise satan's head, that is, destroy his power (Gen. 3:15).

When Jesus came, our calendar started over. It changed from B.C. to A.D. When Jesus came, time began again. That was no accident. Life begins, not at 40, but with the acceptance of Jesus Christ in your heart as your personal Lord and Savior.

PRODIGAL SON—
AN EXAMPLE OF STARTING OVER

The prodigal son was a young man who had it made. His father had lots of money and a big house.

Although the son had work he could do to help manage his father's possessions, he wanted his share of his inheritance, and said, "Dad, I want my inheritance now." His inheritance was to be given to him after his father died, but he said, "I want it *now*." (See Luke 15:11-32.)

His dad gave him the inheritance that would have been his later and he went away and squandered it on wicked living and wild parties. The young man turned away from the covenant of his father. After he blew all of his money and lost all of his friends, he found himself alone.

He had no money, no transportation, no one to go to, so he ended up selling himself to a pig farmer. He was a covenant child of Abraham and in that covenant, there were certain things he was not supposed to eat, but now he filled his belly with the hog slop, because he had no other food.

Many people who criticize Christianity have said, "People only come to God when they are desperate." That's a pretty accurate criticism. But some people have enough sense to recognize it before they get to the bottom of the pigpen!

The prodigal son had a need when he was in his father's house, but he didn't recognize it until everything was stripped away. The wonderful thing about God is, His mercy will accept you back.

Lamentations 3:22-23 says:

"Through the Lord's mercies we are not consumed, because His compassions fail not. They are new every morning, great is Your faithfulness."

The young man began thinking about his circumstances, and he thought, *"Dad has people working for him who have better to eat than I have. They have a better place to live. I'm going back to my dad and say, 'Dad, I've rejected you. I've taken the inheritance, but would you take me back as a servant?'"* The prodigal came home basically because he had physical needs in his life.

God will meet your needs and He will heal your body. There are many prodigals who come home because they need healing in their body and they have other physical needs to be met.

The goodness of God is, *"He makes His sun rise on the evil and on the good, and sends rain on the just and on the unjust"* (Matt. 5:45). He is not just kind to Christians. God is kind to all. God is the giver of every good and perfect gift (James 1:17). Romans 2:4 says, *"The goodness of God leads you to repentance."*

When the prodigal son came home just to get something to eat, he got something he didn't expect. He got a renewed relationship with his father. Dad was sitting on the front porch, looking down the lane when suddenly he saw his son dragging home, clothes torn and dirty.

When the father saw him, he took off running toward his son. That's the picture of how the heavenly Father feels about you, even if you've been a prodigal. He is running toward you, always compassionate and always reaching out.

The father ran and threw his arms around his smelly son and kissed him. He didn't say, "All right, prove yourself." He didn't hold him at arm's length. He loved him. He put a ring on his finger, shoes on his feet, and a robe on his back and told his servants to kill the fatted calf—we're going to have prime rib tonight! My son who was dead is alive. He was lost, but now he's found. Let's rejoice and make merry. (See Luke 15:22-24.)

The prodigal son is a picture of what happens in heaven when one person repents and comes back to God.

EVEN IF YOU HAVE FAILED, IT'S NOT OVER!

You may feel like you can't start over because you've denied the Lord, you've walked away from Him, or you've failed Him. Peter denied Jesus three times. He cursed Him. He denied that he even knew His name. In spite of his failure we hear an angel saying to the three women at the empty tomb on the very morning of Jesus, *resurrection, "Go, tell His disciples and Peter that He is going before you into Galilee; there you will see Him, as He said to you"* (Mark 16:7).

Why did the angel say, "Tell the disciples *and* Peter?" Because *Jesus had a destiny for Peter* who had failed just a few days earlier. In the 40-day period that Jesus showed Himself to His disciples, He showed Peter that He had a plan for his life and that, just because he had failed, it wasn't over!

On the Day of Pentecost, of all the disciples who could have preached, guess who God chose? Peter, the one who failed. God didn't see him as a failure! He gave Peter a new start! Hallelujah! He will do the same for you!

STARTING OVER IN YOUR DEVOTIONAL LIFE

One area in which many people need to start over is their personal devotions with God on a daily basis. By personal devotions, I mean a time during the day that you set aside to pray and seek the Lord, to read the Bible, to listen to God, to repent and confess your sins before God, to pray for other people, to draw strength from Him, and to worship Him.

After a period of time without strong daily devotions with God, some people lose their momentum. You can't live in victory unless you are spending daily time with Jesus. No matter how much you know, the knowledge you have gained in the past will not help you unless it is applied to the present.

Things that are known are often forgotten or sit idle in a corner unless that knowledge is refreshed by the Holy Spirit on a daily basis. When you open yourself up to God on a daily basis, you can face your day and the circumstances that arise. The Holy Spirit will bring to your remembrance the knowledge and information that are needed, and He will enable you, by His wisdom, to know how to apply that knowledge.

Billy Graham, a man who has shaken our world for God's glory, made this statement about our daily devotional time: Nothing can take the place of a daily devotional time with Christ. Your quiet time, prayer time, and time in the Word are absolutely essential for a happy Christian life. It will make the difference between success and failure in your Christian life.

I believe Christians don't need as much new knowledge as they need the application of the knowledge they've already received. This is what happens in a daily time with God.

If you pray, read the Word, and seek God every day, you'll be able to break any demonic influence that tries to come at you. Jesus wants to free you every day from the negative, demonic things that try to come on you in wrong attitudes, thoughts, imaginations, or feelings.

Daily communion with God is an absolute must for you to live in victory. If all you get spiritually is what you receive on Sunday, then you'll be up and down week after week.

It is possible you paused or stopped your devotional time because bad things happened and trials and troubles came. Maybe you received an unexpected hit. Instead of turning to God, you tried to work it out by your own effort.

On the other hand, it's possible you stopped your daily devotional time because of good times. "Everything is fine. I don't need prayer. I don't need to commit myself to God. I'll wait until later."

Maybe you thought, *I've got big business deals going today,* and day after day, devotions are pushed aside until they are off in the distance somewhere. I have good news for you. You can start over!

Steve Davis, former Oklahoma University football quarterback, said, "My greatest battle in life wasn't the linebackers of Nebraska, but it's the daily fight with the devil to maintain a quiet time with God."

Satan will try to keep you from a quiet time through the lust of the flesh, the lust of the eyes, the pride of life, the cares of the world, the drive for riches, or through affliction, tribulation, and persecution. If the devil can destroy this citadel of strength, he can take the fort!

Start over today by setting aside time alone with God. Get your Bible and read, meditate, and confess the promises of God's Word. Then, pray and listen to the Holy Spirit. Pour your heart out to Jesus. It's a new day!

For I know the thoughts that I think toward you, says the Lord, thoughts of peace and not of evil, to give you a future and a hope.

Jeremiah 29:11

"The glory of this latter temple shall be greater than the former," says the Lord of hosts. "And in this place I will give peace," says the Lord of hosts.

Haggai 2:9

Joseph said, "But as for you, you meant evil against me; but God meant it for good, in order to bring it about as it is this day, to save many people alive."

Genesis 50:20

Chapter 6

NEVER GIVE UP!
GET BACK UP!

As Christians, we don't play nine-inning games as in baseball—we play until we win. Since God is the Umpire, we can step up to the plate and bat again!

Think of Joni Eareckson Tada, who, because of a diving injury, has been a quadriplegic for many years. She could have buried herself in remorse and regret for the rest of her life. She could have cursed the day that the accident happened and lived in hate and bitterness. Instead, with God's help and direction, she turned her situation around. As an author she has encouraged thousands.

With a paint brush in her teeth, she paints beautiful pictures. She has inspired many people to believe that God is still a good God and that He can use them, even though they may not have the use of all of their limbs or may be handicapped in another way. She has exemplified the fact that you don't have to be handicapped in your spirit just because you are limited physically.

When Abraham Lincoln was 22 years old, he failed in business. When he was 23, he ran for the legislature and lost. When he was 24, he failed in business again. The following year he was elected to the legislature. When he was 26, his sweetheart died. At the age of 27, he had a nervous breakdown. When he was 29, he was defeated for the post of Speaker of the House in the State Legislature. When he was 31, he was defeated as Elector. When he was 34, he ran for Congress and lost. At the age of 37, he ran for Congress and finally won. Two years later, he ran again and lost his seat in Congress. At the age of 46, he ran for the U.S. Senate and lost. The following year he ran for Vice President and lost that, too. He ran for the Senate again, and again lost. Finally, at the age of 51, Abraham Lincoln was elected President of the United States.[1]

The devil will quickly tell you, "That's three strikes. You've blown it. You're out." That could have happened in Joseph's life: "You blew it with your brothers. You blew it with Potiphar's wife. You were imprisoned and forgotten. Three strikes and you are out!" Joseph's brothers took his coat, but they couldn't take his dream!

Don't give up! You could be one step away from your miracle. The darkest point in any night is right before the morning dawn. The sun will rise again!

ORAL ROBERTS DIDN'T GIVE UP!

As a teenager, Oral Roberts ran away from home. He played basketball, he had a job, and he studied law books into the late hours of the night. He pressed his body so hard that he developed tuberculosis, which was a common affliction for many of the Indian people in the 1930s.

When he collapsed on the basketball court, his dreams appeared to be over, because at that time, there was no cure for tuberculosis. Usually, the people who had it went to the sanatorium or to the graveyard, and he was on his way.

Doctors shook their heads and said, "It's all over. There is no hope." Ministers said, "It will only be a little while longer, and God will take you home." Oral Roberts didn't want to go home. He began to curse it and rehearse it, and a deep bitterness got inside of his heart. But the good news is, he had a praying mama and daddy who wouldn't give up!

One evening a transformation took place in his life as his father prayed. Oral looked up into his father's face as he was praying for him at the end of his bed. Instead of seeing his father's face, he saw the face of Jesus. At that moment, he gave his heart totally to Jesus Christ.

Oral's sister came to see him and spoke seven words that changed his life: "Oral, God is going to heal you." Faith for healing ignited in his heart.

Then his brother Elmer, with a borrowed car and 35 cents worth of gas, came and drove him to a meeting where a divorced man was praying for the sick. In one divine moment, when almost everyone else was gone and Oral was the last one to be prayed for, the man of God laid his hands on him and said, "You foul, tormenting disease, I command you, come out in the name of Jesus." Oral felt air and healing power go into his lungs.

The scars of tuberculosis and the loss that Brother Roberts went through during those months of dying and then the reversal when he released his faith for healing became the platform for a world-wide healing ministry.

Perhaps your life has been scarred from an abortion, drugs, alcohol, or some other hit. What the enemy has meant for evil, God can turn for your good. It can be your platform for sharing the Good

News of Jesus Christ's saving, delivering, and healing power with others.

DAVE ROEVER DIDN'T GIVE UP!

Think of Dave Roever who had half of his face blown off by a phosphorous hand grenade in Vietnam. Fire from the phosphorous burned his entire body. Neither he nor his hospital roommate was recognizable.

His buddy's wife walked into the ward, checked the name tag to be sure it was her husband, took her wedding ring off, and threw it on the bed and said good-bye. When Dave Roever's wife came to the hospital, she also had to check the name tag to be sure it was her husband. As she looked down and kissed his cheek, she said, "I love you, Davey."

Out of that burn unit came the number one public school assembly speaker in America. Dave Roever travels across the nation inspiring young people to rise out of the ashes of defeat, and challenging them not to be bound by drugs, alcohol, and immorality.

REACH FOR THE PRIZE OF THE HIGH CALLING

Some people are nursing scars from divorce, rejection, or time spent in jail. Remember, you aren't the first person to experience these types of scars. Quit nursing and rehearsing them and cursing the people who contributed to them. Start believing, "God has an upward call for me. It is the prize of the high calling of God in Christ Jesus, and I will reach for it and attain it!"

In writing to the Philippians from his prison cell, Paul said:

> But I want you to know, brethren, that the things which happened to me have actually turned out for the furtherance of the gospel,
>
> So that it has become evident to the whole palace guard, and to all the rest, that my chains are in Christ;
>
> And most of the brethren in the Lord, having become confident by my chains, are much more bold to speak the word without fear...
>
> In nothing I shall be ashamed, but with all boldness, as always, so now also Christ will be magnified in my body, whether by life or by death. (Philippians 1:12-14,20)

Paul was saying, "Cheer up! I have made a choice to rejoice regardless of my natural circumstances!"

You can praise your way through the hits and storms of life. Jesus had to get through many storms and hits. In one particular situation, there was a demon-possessed man on the other side of the lake. In most cases, hits and storms come to stop you from reaching the goals God has for you. They come to get you to give up. They come to get you to take an easier pathway so you'll miss the plan of God.

The devil is a cunning, clever schemer. He realizes God is moving on the earth through the Holy Spirit, imparting divine direction to His servants and telling them what to do. Therefore, if he can distract God's servants from doing His will, he will abort God's plan in the earth.

That is exactly what happened to Adam and Eve in the Garden. God intended to rule the earth through Adam and Eve. Satan came to get them off track and turn them away. His strategy hasn't changed. He's coming against you for the same purpose.

Now, storms and hits will come in life, but just because you have some challenges doesn't mean you're not in the will of God. I've rejoiced in that thought many times in my life, and particularly during the most recent altercation when I was punched in the eye during an altar call.

Stay with it. Keep believing God! Continue speaking the Word. The harvest you will reap is worth the price you have to pay to get it!

KEEP YOUR EYES ON THE END GOAL: JESUS!

When you're weary and the storm in your life has been going on for a long time, keep your focus on Jesus:

Looking unto Jesus, the author and finisher of our faith, who for the joy that was set before Him endured the cross, despising the shame, and has sat down at the right hand of the throne of God. (Hebrews 12:2)

God is saying to us that we shouldn't be overly concerned about the obstacles we're going through. Look what Jesus had to go through to reach His goal. Keep your eyes on the end goal. His name is JESUS! We're not just going toward a thing. We're going toward a Person! We're going toward the fulfillment of His will in our lives. We're going toward the completion of His plans for us.

Isaiah 40:31 says:

But those who wait on the Lord shall renew their strength; they shall mount up with wings like eagles, they shall run and not be weary, they shall walk and not faint.

Those who are waiting upon the Lord will not quit! Waiting upon the Lord is ministering unto Him, serving, blessing, praising, and worshiping Him, and waiting in His presence. As you minister to the Lord, He will impart strength to you.

An eagle rides above a storm. It is time that we mount up with wings as eagles and take hold of God's power, strength, and grace. Its time to begin to praise and worship and thank Him, no matter what the storm, the obstacle, the hit, or how you've been defeated or failed in the past. We've all faced it and we've all missed it. Let go of it now and leave it behind.

Let's go on with God, rising above every hit. Let's ride on the winds of the Spirit, like the eagle! Hallelujah!

I pray for the Father to strengthen and encourage you to the point that you are fully confident that no matter what storm or hit comes your way, you're praising on through to victory in the name of Jesus.

ENDNOTE

1. Paul Stirling Hagerman, *It's a Weird World*, (Sterling Publishing Co., Inc., Nov. 1, 1990), 74.

Rejoice in the Lord always. Again I will say, rejoice!

Philippians 4:4

In everything give thanks; for this is the will of God in Christ Jesus for you.

1 Thessalonians 5:18

Chapter 7

A LIFESTYLE OF PRAISE
AND THANKSGIVING

H EBREWS 13:15 is a powerful word regarding the
kind of lifestyle we are to be living: *"Therefore
by Him let us continually offer the sacrifice of praise to
God, that is, the fruit of our lips, giving thanks to His
name."*

Are you living a lifestyle of praise and thanksgiving? What is your personality like and how do
you respond to difficulty? Melancholy? Cool?
Angry? Would anyone ever accuse you of being a
praiser? Not just from *your* standpoint, but from
their standpoint? Could you be implicated for being
a thanks-giver?

The Old Testament sacrifices involved offering calves, bulls, or goats, laying them on the altar, putting incense on them, and then burning them. The fragrance would then go up before God. This was symbolic of the New Testament sacrifice of praise and worship. In the New Testament Jesus became our sacrifice.

Hebrews 13:15 says, *"By Him* [Jesus] *let us continually offer the sacrifice of praise to God, that is, the fruit of our lips...."* Today, we bring the calves, bulls, and goats of our lips, our words, to the altar. They float up to God as sweet incense and are accepted in His presence as praise and worship. The Old and New Testament fit together perfectly, the Old foreshadowing what the New would bring.

How often are we to offer this sacrifice? *"Let us continually offer the sacrifice of praise to God ..."* (v. 15). Does that include Monday morning? How about in the middle of your week? At school? On the job? When you are cooking? When you are eating the cooking? Or when you are doing the dishes? *Continually offering praise.* This means it's a decision or a choice of your will to praise the Lord at all times.

To whom are we to offer the sacrifice of praise? To God. Today, the praise and honor of many people goes to the business tycoon, the guy who is making piles of money. For others it's a sports hero, the one who kicks the field goal, catches the pass, scores the goal, knocks the homerun, or shoots the basket. For others it's a rock star or a country music singer. There's only One who deserves our praise and His name is *JESUS*!

You see, God gave His Son, Jesus gave His life, and He sent the Holy Spirit to indwell us. Today, as born-again believers, we have been delivered from hell because of the mercy of God. The Bible says the penalty for sin is eternal death, but God intervened and sent His Son. Jesus gave His blood. For those who will receive Jesus Christ as their Savior and Lord, they will receive eternal life with Him. In John 14:6, Jesus said, *"I am the way, the truth, and the life. No one comes to the Father except through Me."*

Some people say, "I don't have anything for which to praise God." You need to have your head examined! Heaven beats hell by a long shot! That's why the Bible says, *"...Rejoice because your names are written in heaven"* (Luke 10:20).

When Jesus entered Jerusalem, all the people were praising Him and the Pharisees said, *"Teacher, rebuke Your disciples"* (Luke 19:39). Jesus said, *"I tell you that if these should keep silent, the stones would immediately cry out"* (v. 40). I don't want any rock replacing me!

Giving thanks to His name (Hebrews 13:15).

Make this confession with me now:

Thank You, Lord, for Your name. By Your name I was saved and delivered. By Your name I have been blessed. By Your name I have joy. Lord, I thank You that Your name has brought peace to my life. Thank You, Lord, by Your name I have guidance, direction, *wisdom, help, and comfort. I am going to thank You, Lord Jesus, for Your name has set me free!*

GENERAL BORISOV, A CONTINUAL PRAISER!

I was preaching in Moscow, Russia, in a Leadership Conference held at a Spirit-filled Baptist church. There was an older distinguished-looking gentleman with white hair who waved at me while I was preaching. At first I didn't recognize him, but while I had someone come to share a testimony, I walked off the platform and I recognized him.

Many years ago when Russia was fighting against Afghanistan, the second highest ranking army general of Russia, a dedicated Communist and atheist who hated God and anything to do with Him, had several of his soldiers witness to him about Jesus Christ. He was so angry about it that he told the KGB to take care of them, which they did.

Later, while on a trip, a missile slammed into the general's helicopter. As the helicopter was spiraling downward toward the mountains of Afghanistan, in a flash it came back to his mind what those men had told him. He cried out to the Lord to save him.

The crash occurred and he was knocked unconscious. When he opened his eyes, wherever they had taken him for medical attention and recovery, he looked around and said, "I didn't think it was heaven and I knew it wasn't hell."

That general, General Slava Borisov, was born again and filled with the Holy Spirit. Through the organization he established in Russia, he is responsible for putting over two million Bibles in the hands of Russian troops and in establishing chapels on some military bases.

Under Communism, the Russians didn't have Christian marriage ceremonies, so General Borisov and his wife just lived together for 30 some years. When he and his wife came to America, he wanted to have a Christian marriage, so I married them in the Prayer Room at Victory Christian Center.

During the Leadership Conference meeting in Moscow, I called General Borisov to the platform and he shared about some of the things that were happening in his life and in his outreach programs. He told of the opportunity he has had to develop a relationship with President George W. Bush.

During the Afghanistan conflict, there was a bounty on his life for $1 million. Because of the successful change of leadership there, today the bounty has been removed. General Borisov visited the Pentagon in Washington, D.C., and met with U.S. generals. He shared his testimony and tears flowed that day within the powerful Pentagon walls. Today there are many prayer meetings going on in the Pentagon with generals and other personnel who love God and are serving Him.

The reason I share about General Borisov is that today he lives in a continual attitude of praise and thanksgiving. Some people have been Christians all of their lives. They have had so many good things to enjoy. Here, on the other hand, is a man who has lived through Communism, suffered through several surgeries after the helicopter crash, and provided comfort to his wife who has gone through some physical difficulties—but he keeps praising the Lord right on through!

TAKING CARE OF BUSINESS

When I talk about a lifestyle of praise and thanksgiving, it is important that I share about the other side of the coin as well. This does not mean you don't take care of business. Sometimes when you teach a truth, people take that one truth and neglect all the other truths. So it doesn't mean that we don't address issues that need to be addressed in our lives. Or if you have oversight in a company, it doesn't mean you don't correct those under your supervision. It doesn't mean you don't correct things in your own life. In other words, while you are correcting, keep on praising! *But don't substitute praise for the things you need to be doing.* If someone needs forgiveness or you need repentance, take care of that business, but praise right on through it.

In whatever you are doing and wherever you are living, praise can become a part of it. I want to encourage you to praise God while you are driving. Keep one hand on the wheel and one eye open! You can praise on the work site or even at a coffee break! Just say, "Excuse me for a moment. I've got to have a praise break!" Sometimes people need a praise break. Tension, worry, anxiety, and pressure attack people. One of the best ways to handle it is with praise, not *for* situations, but *in* the midst of them.

PURSUING A PRAISE AND THANKSGIVING LIFESTYLE

God has called us to live in a lifestyle of praise and thanksgiving. You are to live in praise, thanksgiving, and worship, just like a fish lives in water. What happens if you take a fish out of water? It will shrivel up and die! That's why some Christians look like they've been pickled or preserved! They have been out of praise so long they don't even know what it is. When you live in that atmosphere, it has an effect on your face! Praise and worship is the environment we were intended to live.

Last year we were in Chelyabinsk and Izhevsk, Russia, preaching. Chelyabinsk is on the eastern side of the Ural Mountains and Izhevsk is on the western side. A couple of weeks before the meeting, a key political official in the city who opposed the preaching of the gospel said, "We are canceling the use of the building they are to be in."

We had spent thousands of dollars in advertising to get the word out about the meetings, so we had to scramble to find a new building. What are you going to do in such a situation? Praise on through! We weren't bitter at the guy who closed the building to us. We weren't going to worry about it. We praised right on through. People found their way to the new site and the Russians worked to redirect the people who showed up at the original site. We ended up with a packed full service in Chelyabinsk.

In another trip to Izhevsk, five days before the meeting, I received a call, "Pastor, there has been an explosion in the building where we are to meet. All the power systems are out." I said, "Let's find another building." You can't get upset or bitter, but you can praise right on through difficulties into victory.

When we were preaching in a huge soccer stadium in Freetown, the capital of Sierra Leone, Bill Turkovich, who had ministered in Sierra Leone many times and knew the culture of the people and what was going on in the country, was our coordinator. We were staying in a home built 50 or 60 years ago. There weren't a lot of nice places to stay in Sierra Leone. At that time the country was in the midst of a civil war.

When it was time to go to the meeting, Bill said, "Pastor, let's wait a little while." I said, "Okay, how long?" "Well, maybe a couple of hours," was his response. In a bit of a panic, I responded, "A couple of hours? The meeting starts soon and we've got to be there." Countering, Bill said, "We need to wait."

I asked him, "What is going on?"

He said, "Everything is okay. They are just fixing a few things."

We found out what they were fixing! There were major demonstrations by opponents of the crusade, and they were burning tires in front of all the entries to the stadium. The army was out fighting with these people in the streets who were of another persuasion. I said, "Lord, just clear the way!"

Two hours later the stadium was filled with people. We had a magnificent service. The civil war in that country had been going on for 11 years. In that meeting, God dealt with us to have the entire congregation stand for over 15 minutes—the crowd was estimated to be between 60,000 and 70,000 people—and I encouraged them to declare, "Jesus is Lord over Sierra Leone and let's praise Him."

Within a few months after the stadium meeting, the rebels laid down their weapons and surrendered. The war was over after 11 years of fighting. There was no natural explanation. There was no major offensive and no additional things happened. It simply was all over. The point is, keep praising on through! God is going to give you victory!

During another trip to Russia, a funny thing happened. After holding a night service at Chelyabinsk we were going to fly over the Ural Mountains to Ishevsk where we were to start a Pastors' Conference the next morning. It was about an hour-and-a-half flight.

The Ural Mountains are over 6,000 feet high with jagged peaks. It was snowing and icing, and we were flying on a plane that was built shortly after or during the Second World War. On our way to the airport, I said, "I pray they've got a deicer on this plane." We walked to the back of the plane and were about to get on when I looked up and there was a guy standing on the wings with a broom! He was the deicer!

This warm feeling came all over me. Talk about praising on through! The owner of the airline flew with us which gave me mixed feelings. One of the greatest moments in my life was when we landed safely at Izhevsk! We made a choice to praise on through!

SERVING THE LORD WITH JOY AND GLADNESS

Deuteronomy 28:45-47 identifies the blessings for obedience and the curses for disobedience, as well as the effect of serving the Lord with joy and gladness. Moses received these statutes from God. If the people would obey God's commands, they would be blessed in the city, blessed in the field, blessed coming and blessed going, the head and not the tail, above and not beneath. But for those who didn't obey God and keep His laws and statutes, the curses would come on them. Moses talks about the curse coming because the people didn't serve the Lord with joy and gladness. I want you to realize this deep down inside—serve with joy and gladness.

Moreover all these curses shall come upon you and pursue and overtake you, until you are destroyed, because you did not obey the voice of the Lord your God, to keep His commandments and His statutes which He commanded you (Deuteronomy 28:45).

You have to understand, it wasn't that God wanted these curses to come on anyone. God was just saying, "If you will obey Me, there is protection, but if you disobey, there is no protection. These curses will come after you and you won't be able to stop them." Sometimes people misread this, thinking God was saying He wanted the curses to come. No, it was a law. In obedience there are blessings, but in disobedience there are curses.

Verse 46 says, *"And they [the curses] shall be upon you for a sign and a wonder, and on your descendants forever."* Imagine, signs and wonders of curses chasing those who are disobedient, as well as their children and their children's children.

Verse 47 is a key: *"Because you did not serve the Lord your God with joy and gladness of heart, for the abundance of everything."* God's will for you is the abundance of everything. Also, His will is that you serve Him with joy and gladness. The Lord said, "These curses will come on you if you don't serve Me with joy and gladness."

It's not just serving the Lord, but it is our attitude that counts. It's time for an "attitude of gratitude," not an attitude of complaining, murmuring, fault-finding, negativism, depression, heaviness, defeat, fear, doubt and unbelief, or doom and gloom. Is it possible that some people today have curses chasing them down because they are not serving the Lord with joy and gladness of heart?

THE NEW TESTAMENT LAW OF LOVE

The Law of Moses was Old Covenant, but there is a law in the New Covenant—the law of love.

In Matthew 22:37-40 Jesus said:

> *You shall love the Lord your God with all your heart, with all your soul, and with all your mind. This is the first and great commandment. And the second is like it: You shall love your neighbor as yourself. On these two commandments hang all the Law and the Prophets.*

It is possible that curses could come upon your life under the New Covenant because you are not serving the Lord with joy and gladness.

Jesus has something better for you than heaviness. He has a garment of praise for you. Isaiah 61:3 tells us that we should replace the spirit of heaviness with the garment of praise. It is your decision to put it on. He has a better life for you. Heaviness is a lifestyle for many people. Some people feel called to be depressed. Others have an anointing to be critical. They're specialists in cutting people down.

For some people, worry, anxiety, and fear have become a lifestyle. What if you change that lifestyle and become a praiser? Maybe you're thinking, *"Well, my mama wasn't like that and my grandma wasn't like that either."* Why don't you start a new generation? There are a lot of brand-new things that come to us when we are new creatures in Christ Jesus. You may have never lived around it, but it is not impossible.

This is why I thought about General Borisov. He was never around praising, joyful people. He was one of the roughest guys in the Russian military. Yet when he found Christ, he became a praiser, one who gives thanks. Today he is as joyful as he can be.

IN EVERYTHING GIVE THANKS!

First Thessalonians 5:18 says, *"In **everything** give thanks; for this is the will of God in Christ Jesus for you."* This doesn't mean to give thanks *for* everything. There are some bad things such as opposition and personal problems that happen that you know are from the devil. But in the situation, you can give thanks that God is still on your side. You can give thanks that He is still on the throne, that He is for you and not against you, and that He has redeemed you by Jesus' blood.

"In everything give thanks; for this is the will of God...." How are you going to know the will of God for your life? If you will give thanks, God has more for you. If you won't give thanks, why should He tell you any more? I'm talking about the known will of God being revealed in your life through an attitude of praise and thanksgiving.

You've got to make up your mind, "I'm going to be a praiser." First Corinthians 15:57 says, *"But thanks be to God, who gives us the victory through our Lord Jesus Christ."* You have already been given the victory. You may look defeated, feel that way, and have problems, but Christ has already defeated death, hell, the grave, satan, and sin. He has given you the victory. It belongs to you. It is yours today. **"Thanks be to God!"**

When you praise Him, you will possess victory. Many people are like Thomas saying, "I'll believe it when I see it." But if you will go ahead and praise Him when it doesn't look like the answer is on the way, you will see victory!

JEHOSHAPHAT AND HIS ARMIES PRAISED THEIR WAY TO VICTORY

Jehoshaphat and the armies of Judah began to praise God and He caused their enemies to fight against one another. Surrounded by three armies there was nowhere to go and no way to overcome the advancing forces. So what caused them to overcome?

First, Jehoshaphat and the inhabitants from all the cities of Judah *"gathered together to ask help from the Lord..."* (2 Chron. 20:4). After they sought the Lord corporately, with Jehoshaphat in the lead, verse 14 says, *"The Spirit of the Lord came upon Jahaziel...."* Then, in verses 15-17 Jahaziel said:

Listen, all you of Judah and you inhabitants of Jerusalem, and you, King Jehoshaphat! Thus says the Lord to you: Do not be afraid nor dismayed because of this great multitude, for the battle is not yours, but God's. Tomorrow go down against them. They will surely come up by the Ascent of Ziz, and you will find them at the end of the brook before the Wilderness of Jeruel. You will not need to fight in this battle. Position yourselves, stand still and see the salvation of the Lord, who is with you, O Judah and Jerusalem! Do not fear or be dismayed;

tomorrow go out against them, for the Lord is with you.

Verse 18 says: *"And Jehoshaphat bowed his head with his face to the ground, and all Judah and the inhabitants of Jerusalem bowed before the Lord, worshiping the Lord."*

Jehoshaphat and his people responded out of a spirit of praise and thanksgiving. However, this wasn't the end of the praise and thanksgiving.

Jehoshaphat appointed *those who should sing to the Lord, and who should praise the beauty of holiness, as they went out before the army and were saying: "Praise the Lord, for His mercy endures forever"* (2 Chron. 20:21). As they sang and praised, the Lord set ambushments against the three armies that were against them and the enemy was defeated! Jehoshaphat and the inhabitants of Judah praised their way to victory!

PRAISE WILL GET YOU AIRBORNE!

Why should we praise God? Because we already know the outcome! Praise will cause the enemy to go into confusion. Praise is what gets you airborne. A lot of people are just taxiing up and down the runway, saying, "I'm a hopin' and a prayin'. You all pray with me." Get off the runway and turn on the praise:

"Lord, I praise You. I thank You that You have redeemed me! You are going to make a way for me where there seems to be no way!" Suddenly, you are airborne and you are on your way!

Second Corinthians 2:14 says, *"Now thanks be to God who always leads us in triumph in Christ...."* You may be in the middle of a problem, but you can thank God that He is causing you to triumph. There is no defeat for you if you will obey God and continually offer praise and thanksgiving to Him for His grace and mercy!

If you are a student struggling with a course, you can say, "Thank You, Lord, You are causing me to triumph through this course. I will never have this class again! Thank You, Lord." I'm so thankful I got through accounting, Hebrew, chemistry, and physics. Thank You, Lord, I will never ever have another class in chemistry or physics. Some people just eat that up. You can have my portion!

BLESS THE LORD, O MY SOUL!

Psalm 103:1-2 says, *"Bless the Lord, O my soul; and all that is within me, bless His holy name! Bless the Lord, O my soul, and forget not all His benefits."*

Sometimes you have to talk to yourself: "Bless the Lord, O my soul." David talked to himself, saying, "Soul, you bless the Lord." *Bless*, means to give thanks and praise. Maybe you need to have a good talk with yourself because you may be down, depressed, and feeling like, I don't want to praise God. You can just say, "Self, you get up and praise God. You're going to bless the Lord whether you want to or not or whether you feel like it or not."

Some people are so wrapped up in the problems, difficulties, and situations they are facing that they have forgotten the benefits. If it will help you, pick up the Book and say, "Lord, I thank You, You have forgiven my sins; healed my diseases; redeemed my life from destruction; crowned me with lovingkindness and tender mercies; satisfied my mouth with good things; and renewed my youth like the eagles." (See Psalm 103:1-5). Thank You, Lord Jesus.

Jesus healed ten lepers, but only one returned to thank Him. Jesus expected ten out of ten to give thanks. But the law of averages is about the same today. About one out of ten come back to say, Lord, I just want to thank You for saving me. Thank You for healing me. Thank You for rescuing me from the pit. Thank You for keeping my feet from falling and my eyes from tears. Thank You for delivering my life. Lord, I want to say thank You. Will you be one of the nine on the take, or will you be like the one who returned to give thanks?

OUR DAUGHTER RUTH PRAISED HER WAY TO COMPLETE VICTORY!

Our daughter Ruth praised on through a situation that happened when she was a student at Oral Roberts University. At the time she was also leading one of Victory's children's church services. She woke up one morning and one side of her face was paralyzed. That week the lesson in children's church was on healing. What do you do? She couldn't talk clearly. She was diagnosed with Bell's palsy, and the doctor said, "In some cases, it goes away in weeks, some in months, others never."

That week Ruthie taught on healing in front of all the kids. Some of them asked her, "What's wrong with you?" Ruthie answered back with great faith saying, "I'm healed." Insisting on a different response, they asked, "Okay, Ruthie, what's really wrong with you?" She responded again, "I said, I'm healed."

Ruthie went to her classes and never changed her schedule. She held fast her confession of faith and just kept praising God. One morning several days later, she woke up and the paralysis was gone! Hallelujah!

PRAISE ON THROUGH!

What are you going to do when you are facing problems and difficulties or you have experienced an unexpected hit? Praise on through! Just keep on praising God! When someone asks, "Well, what are you going to do now?" Tell them what you're going to do: "I'm going to praise right on through the problem! It has worked in the past, it's working right now, and it will work in the future. Why? Because Jesus is worthy of my praise. He deserves my praise. He is the One who is going to be glorified and honored all the way through."

REASONS WHY SOME PEOPLE DON'T PRAISE

Why don't people praise the Lord and give thanks on a regular basis? I believe the number one reason is *pride*. People think they are doing everything themselves. They wonder, why should I give God praise? I mean, what has He done for me anyway? Arrogance, ego, smugness, and pride keep many from giving thanks and praise to God.

Another reason people don't praise the Lord is *self-centeredness*. Many people are so into themselves—their job, school, activities, friends, what they're thinking and what people are thinking about them, what they are going to wear, what they are going to drive, and where they are going to live. They are so wrapped up in themselves that they don't have time to think about giving God praise.

For others, *fear or peer pressure* are reasons they don't praise the Lord,. What would other people think if I praise God, thank Him, and mention His name out loud? Then there are people who are just plain *ungrateful*.

You have to make a decision to be a praiser. When you realize how low the pit was you came out of and how Jesus didn't deserve to die, He didn't deserve the scars and nails in His hands and feet, a crown of thorns on His head, or the stripes on His back, your attitude about praise will change. Jesus took all of this because He loves you and me and He stood in our place, taking the punishment of sin for us. No person or object deserves the praise and honor that belong to God alone. He deserves our praise.

No rock star ever died on the cross for you and me. No great athlete is going to lay his life down for you and me. These "worldly stars" don't even know who we are, yet the Bible says that Jesus knows the number of hairs on our head (Matt. 10:30). He knows our address, He loves us, and before we were ever born, He cared about us. Jesus is interceding in heaven right now for you and me.

It is such an awesome realization to understand that we have the *privilege* of praising Him. This is the style of our life. This is when we get in the water and we swim. Why? *Praise is the element in which we were born to live.*

Do you know that if you don't put oil on an engine, it grinds? There are a lot of people who are cranky, grinding, and sputtering right now because they don't have the oil of praise in their lives. You are to flow in an atmosphere of worship and praise.

You have to take care of business, be attentive, respond to things, deal with issues, and correct things in your life. If you are in an oversight position, you have to address issues when things are not right. But in the middle of all that you are doing, you can still keep an attitude of praise and thanksgiving. It's up to you to choose to do that!

"He is no fool who gives up what he cannot keep to gain that which he cannot lose."

—Jim Elliot

"People who do not know the Lord ask why in the world we waste our lives as missionaries. They forget that they too are expending their lives...and when the bubble has burst, they will have nothing of eternal significance to show for the years they have wasted."

—Nate Saint

"Character cannot be developed in ease and quiet. Only through experience of trial and suffering can the soul be strengthened, ambition inspired, and success achieved."

—Helen Keller

Chapter 8

KNOCKED DOWN, BUT NOT OUT—INSPIRATIONAL STORIES OF OVERCOMERS

THROUGHOUT the ages, in every sphere of life, there have been those who have overcome failure. They have snatched victory out of the jaws of defeat. In this chapter you will read stories of those who discovered the power to turn defeat into victory. It is my prayer that these stories will inspire you in your times of darkness.

FINDING GRACE IN A COMMUNIST PRISON

Don Milam and his wife, Micki, had prepared to go to Mozambique as missionaries and arrived in

Maputo, Mozambique, in 1972. They knew that the Portuguese colonialists had been in an ongoing struggle with freedom fighters in the North of this beautiful country. Frelimo, the communist-backed rebel group, had been waging a guerrilla-type war for independence and it had been going on for so long, people took it in stride. In the South, where the Milams lived in the capital city, life went on in relatively normal fashion. They saw little fear in the people they worked among or in other missionaries.

In 1974 the unimaginable happened. The military in Portugal successfully affected a coup d'etat against the government, and the first thing the new junta did was give independence to their three African colonies. A year later, in June 1975, Frelimo celebrated Mozambique's independence with jeeps of soldiers firing their automatic weapons into the air in the streets of Lourenco Marques.

At the urging of the U.S. Consulate, most American missionaries left, but Don and Micki and their staff sought direction from the Lord and felt it was right for them to stay. The people they had been ministering to and had come to love had no place to go for sanctuary. They would not leave them.

One month after Independence Day, Don was arrested and taken to the police station. He was questioned for six hours and had no way of knowing that two of his staff workers were being interrogated in another room. Later that evening he was put in a military jeep and driven home. Several soldiers woke his wife and children as they searched their house, waving their weapons.

Don didn't know what they were looking for and had only a minute to quickly whisper to Micki that it would be all right—that this was just a big misunderstanding, and once they realized it, things would be fine.

By then it was about ten o'clock at night, and Don was brusquely ordered back outside and into the jeep. He was taken to an ominous-looking military prison. Arriving in the dark of night, he was processed and led to cell number six in prison block A. Dazed, he found himself secured with two other prisoners.

"Oh God, where are You?" he cried out. No answer seemed to come. But a certain peace drifted into the cell.

That was the first of 300 nights Don spent in that dark, fear-filled, concrete prison. He had prepared his whole adult life to serve the Lord in this very country where he was now imprisoned. His lifelong dream had turned into a nightmare. Where was God, and how could He let this happen? His earlier confidence that this was all a mistake began to evaporate. What was going to happen to Micki and his three small children with chaos and violence escalating in the destabilized country? Horror stories of the unrestrained actions of "guerrillas turned policemen" filtered into the prison daily.

Gradually he settled into the daily routine of prison life. From the very first day, the prison guards expressed great antipathy for all the foreigners under their care. The first morning he was dragged by the soldiers into the mess hall and ordered to take off his shoes, get on his knees, and wash the floor with a brush. This was the first of many humiliations. He came to dread the times when the whole prison population was brought together and made to watch while certain inmates were beaten and tortured. As a sheltered American, he was shocked at the total disregard for human life of these cruel jailers.

Adding to his ragged emotional state of mind was the fear for his family living on the outside. They were trying to get by in those tumultuous days when single women were being targeted by roving bands of ex-guerrillas, now soldiers. Food was scarce and homes were being broken into and robbed. On one stormy night while his wife and children were sleeping, their home was broken into and all their belongings were stolen. Milam's mind was racked with a deep sense of helplessness to protect them.

In the midst of the dark cloud of fear and uncertainty that hung over him, he became aware of a quiet but powerful energy at work in him. This was the first time he experientially came to know the force we call grace—the empowering presence. While he was not always conscious of this power, it was there and it was working. Grace was empowering him for this moment. At times he could literally feel the warmth of God's presence sweeping over the cold gripping his soul.

The Frelimo soldiers who were the official guards over the prison looked for ways to frighten and humiliate the foreigners. Toward the end of his time in prison, their fear tactics increased. One Sunday they burst into his cell and hauled him and six or seven other prisoners into the prison courtyard. Handing each one of them a shovel and herding them to the middle of the courtyard, they were sharply commanded to start digging.

After digging for nearly four hours they stood in a massive hole whose lip was over their heads. During this entire time the soldiers, who were high on marijuana, yelled and waved their AK-47s threateningly over their heads. Finally they screamed at them to climb up out of the hole, whereupon they lined them up with the gaping hole at their heels and their fierce countenances in front. Milan wondered if this might be the end. He was never going home; he was never going to see his family again.

With their eyes tightly closed, they heard the frightening sound of weapons being loaded. He stood resigned, waiting for the bullets that would end the horror. Nothing! Suddenly a wild fit of laughter broke the silence. Immediately they started shoving the prisoners toward the prison doors. It took Don some time to realize that he was still alive. He had survived another life-threatening encounter in this nightmare. God had been there with him. When he thought his life would end, it had begun all over again with a new sense of His empowering presence with him.

It was the power of God's wonderful grace—a very real power outside himself that was strengthening him in those awful days. Grace was there, wrapping him in a warm embrace.

The storm finally passed. After ten months of never knowing if he was going to live or die, in May 1976 he was expelled from Mozambique under miraculous circumstances. He learned during those days that, though it seems like there is no way to get out of our trouble, there is a "higher power" present with us, protecting us and bringing us back into the light. God will help those who have been knocked down and will raise them up.

FIVE DEATHS THAT ROCKED THE WORLD

Of all tragedies, death for nothing could be considered the greatest *knock down. But even in death, a knock down is not necessarily a knock out.* Sometimes, sweet incense emerges out of the darkness of death.

Many people thought it was a tragic waste of life when Nate Saint, Ed McCully, Jim Elliot, and Peter Fleming, and Roger Youderian died while preaching the Gospel to the Auca Indians. Often, the blood of the martyrs becomes the seed of the Church. Five of the most famous missionaries of the Church proved this point when they laid down their lives in the jungles of Ecuador. Out of their tragic deaths the Gospel took hold among the Aucas.

In the dense rain forests of Ecuador, on the Pacific side of the Andes Mountains, lives a tribe of Indians who call themselves the Huaorani. Huaorani means *people* in their language, Huao. Their neighbors, though, call them the Aucas—meaning *savages* in Quechua.

For many generations this tribe had been completely isolated from the outside world, disposed to kill any stranger on sight, and feared even by their head-hunting neighbors, the Jivaro tribe.[1] Five missionaries entered this jungle, never to return.

Nate Saint was their pilot. He had taken flying lessons in high school and served in the U.S. Air Force in World War II. After the war, he enrolled in Wheaton College to prepare for foreign mission work but he dropped out to join the Missionary Aviation Fellowship. Saint established a base at Shell Mera (an abandoned oil exploration camp in Ecuador) in September 1948, and flew short hops to keep missionaries supplied with medicines, mail, and things they needed in their work in foreign countries.

The other three, Ed McCully, Jim Elliot, and Peter Fleming, all Plymouth Brethren, went to Ecuador in 1952 to work for CMML (Christian Missions in Many Lands).

Ed McCully had been a football and track star at Wheaton College, and president of his senior class. After graduating from Wheaton, he enrolled in Marquette College to study law, but dropped out to go to Ecuador. He and his wife, Marilou, worked with the Quechuas tribe at Arajuno, a base near the Huaorani.

Jim Elliot was an honors graduate at Wheaton College, where he had been a debater, public speaker, and champion wrestler. In Ecuador, he married Elisabeth Howard and they served as paramedics, tending to broken arms, malaria, snakebites, teaching literacy and sanitation, and writing books in Quechua.

Peter Fleming was from the University of Washington, an honor student and linguist, married to Olive. Together they ran a literacy program among the Quechuas.

Roger Youderian was from rural Montana, a former paratrooper who had fought in the Battle of the Bulge and had been in General Eisenhower's honor guard. His jungle savvy was important to the team's success.[2]

All five were aware of the risk they were taking but they were committed to the divine call on their lives—even though they all had families. They prepared themselves to lessen the risks and tried to learn about the Huaorani as much as possible from as many as possible.

They learned several Huao words and phrases from a Huao girl named Dayuma who had fled almost certain death and lived "within civilization." Nate's sister, Rachel, with whom Dayuma lived, kept studying the Huao language believing that God would let her live with the tribe and teach God's truths to her people.

The men's plan was to locate themselves in an old oil station that was abandoned because it was considered too dangerous for oil personnel. It was close to the Auca tribe and had a small airstrip.

To get to Shandia they had to take a plane to the nearest village. Nate was their pilot. Just east of the ancient Inca Empire, they landed in the nearby village and hiked for two hours through jungle and swamplands to get to Shandia.

When they arrived at Shandia, Pete and Jim made contact with the Quechua Indians. Ed and his wife, Marilou, joined Pete and Jim in Shandia after completing six months of Spanish training in Quito. Nate and his wife also joined them. Together they built a mission station, a small medical station, a few houses for the missionaries to live in, and a small airstrip, which all took about a year. After all that had been accomplished, the missionaries had their first Bible conference with the Quechuas. Unfortunately, during the rainy season, a flood wiped out everything that they had built during their first year.

With Nate's help as the pilot, the men discovered the first Auca huts. As the plans for contact with the Aucas continued, Roger Youderian, a young missionary, was asked to join them. The men's first attempt to contact them was by airplane. Nate flew the plane around the camp while the men shouted friendship words in the Auca language through a loud speaker. They dropped gifts baskets filled with beads, cloths, machetes, and a photograph of each man. The Aucas realized they were friendly and allowed them to land on an island they called Palm

Beach. The Aucas responded by presenting a parrot and feathered headdresses.[3]

Encouraged by this progress and after three to four months of gift dropping, they decided to make a base along the Curray River on Palm Beach. After a week had passed, four Aucas unexpectedly came to Palm Beach. The five men gave them food and gifts as a sign of peace.

After a few days of transferring their equipment to their new campsite they set up shelter. When they were settled in they shouted Auca phrases into the jungle to let the Aucas know they were there. The men were always ready for visits from the Auca and carried firearms, but they made an agreement not to use their weapons unless necessary. Four days later two Auca women and a man appeared on the other side of the river at the edge of the jungle. Stunned, the missionaries started frantically shouting out phrases in the Auca language. The man replied speaking in his own language and frequently pointing at one of the girls. Jim immediately jumped into the river and swam across.

Frightened and a bit surprised the Aucas backed up into the jungle.

Finally after a little persuasion, they were able to convince them to come into their camp.

When they got back to their campsite, the missionaries showed the Indians modern things such as rubber bands, balloons, and balls. Then they had lunch of hamburgers with mustard. Toward the end of the visit, the Indians showed signs that they wanted to stay the night on the beach with them. The missionaries hospitably set up a hut and said that they could sleep there for the night.

Encouraged by this visit, the men felt that it was time to go into the Auca village and try to minister to them. On the morning of January 8, 1955, after numerous songs of praise and considerable prayer, the men radioed their wives saying that they were going to the village and would radio them at about 4:30. "Operation Auca" was under way.

As Nate and Ed were flying back to Shell Mera they saw a group of 20 or 30 Aucas going toward Palm Beach. As soon as they saw them, they got very excited, turned around and landed at Palm Beach. They shouted, "Guys, the Aucas are coming!" As soon as the three others heard that, they flew into action straightening up their camp. Little did these five men know that this would be their last few hours of life. The last radio contact they made with Shell Mera was Jim calling his wife saying, "We'll call you back in three hours."

The women back at the base prayed constantly for their husbands' time with the Aucas to be successful and asking God to keep them safe. At 4:30 there was no contact, which immediately put the women in alarm. An hour later helicopters and planes from the Ecuadorian Air Force, the United States Army, Air Force and Navy swarmed along the Curray River looking for the missionaries.

Finally, one of the helicopter pilots radioed in saying that their bodies had been found on the beach. Jim Elliot's body was found downstream with three others. Their bodies had been brutally pierced with spears and hacked with machetes. All of the airplane's fabric had been ripped off as if they had tried to kill the plane. Nate's watch stopped at 3:12 p.m. so it was concluded that the Indians had attacked them at that time. Their wives received the news and replied, "The Lord has closed our hearts to grief and hysteria, and filled in with His perfect peace."

The blood of the martyr is the seed of the Church.

—Tertullian

After the brutal deaths of five brave men, the effort to reach the Huaorani was not abandoned but rather intensified. Within three weeks, Johnny Keenan, another pilot of the Ecuador Mission, was continuing the flights over the Auca village. More than 20 fliers from the United States promptly applied to take Nate's place. More than 1,000 college students volunteered for foreign missions in direct response to the story of the Five Martyrs. In Ecuador, attendance by Indians at the mission stations, schools, and church services reached record levels, and the number of conversions skyrocketed.

Four years later, in 1959, Nate's sister, Rachel, and Jim Elliot's widow, Elisabeth, made contact with the Auca tribe. Rachel, called "Star" by the Waodani, lived with the people for three decades after her brother's martyrdom. She helped translate the Bible into their language. When she died of cancer in 1994, Waodani leaders quickly invited Steve, Rachel's nephew, who had spent school vacations in the jungle, to take her place.

Steve Saint spent summers there from the age of 9. He was "adopted" by Mincaye, the man who killed his father. In 1994, Mincaye asked Steve to help the tribe become less dependent on foreigners. Steve founded the Indigenous People's Technology and Education Center that adapts dentistry and other skills for non-industrial cultures.[4]

After moving his family to Ecuador, Steve discovered that the Waodani were still dependent on foreign money and missionaries to survive. Over the next few years Steve dedicated himself to making the Waodani independent by opening an Education Center for the Waodani.

In January 2006, over 50 years after the massacre, a film, *End of the Spear*, was released telling the story about these brave men and women dedicated to spreading the Gospel.

The five men on the beach were ready to die and their deaths were not in vain. They were knocked down but even death was not able to knock them out. Through the efforts of the families they left behind, the Auca turned Huaorani discovered Christian forgiveness. A whole new generation of missionaries has been raised up, inspired by these five men who dared to take the Gospel where no man had gone before.

HELEN KELLER

Helen Adams Keller was born on June 27, 1880, in Tuscumbia, a small rural town in Northwest Alabama, United States. When she was 19 months old, she suffered from meningitis and became blind and deaf as a result. The doctors of the time called it "brain fever," while modern doctors think it may have been scarlet fever or meningitis.

Whatever the illness, Helen was, for many days, expected to die. When, eventually, the fever subsided, Helen's family rejoiced believing their daughter would be well again. However, Helen's mother soon noticed how her daughter was failing to respond when the dinner bell rang or when she passed her hand in front of her daughter's eyes. It became apparent that Helen's illness had left her both blind and deaf.[5]

Helen was a very bright child. She became very frustrated because she couldn't talk. She became very angry and would throw temper tantrums. As she grew up, she learned to accomplish tiny errands, but she also realized that she was missing something. "Sometimes," she later wrote, "I stood between two persons who were conversing and touched their lips. I could not understand, and was vexed. I moved my lips and gesticulated frantically without result. This made me so angry at times that I kicked and screamed until I was exhausted."[6]

The family was devastated by Helen's condition and desperate to find a way out of the tragedy that had struck their home. By the time Helen was 6 years old, the problem was proving to be too much for them. After some research her mom, Kate, decided to travel to Baltimore to visit a specialist. It was there that their worst fears were confirmed. Helen would never see or hear again. However, the doctor did suggest that there was someone local who was teaching deaf children. We know this person as the inventor of the telephone, Alexander Graham Bell. In addition to being a great inventor, Bell had a great passion to help blind people live successively in their world.

After Kate discussed Helen's situation with Mr. Bell, he recommended that she take Helen to see Michael Anagnos, director of the Perkins Institution and Massachusetts Asylum for the Blind. Bell was certain that once she reached him he would be able to recommend someone to help.

Anagnos, upon considering Helen's situation, made a life-changing recommendation. He sent them to a former pupil, Anne Sullivan. Miss Sullivan herself had been blind, but had an operation that gave her back her sight. Anne understood what Helen was feeling and she became the perfect partner for Helen. Their friendship would last for a lifetime.

Immediately Anne began to work with Helen teaching her how to finger spell. Anne taught Helen the signs for the letters of the alphabet and then she began to communicate with Helen by spelling words on her hand. Helen Keller became the first blind-deaf person to effectively communicate with a world in which vision and sound are of such importance.

It was difficult for Helen to capture the meaning of this finger language but everything was about to change. Helen had until now not yet fully understood the meaning of words. On April 5, 1887, Anne took Helen outside to a water pump.

As Anne pumped the water over Helen's hand, Anne spelled out the word *water* in the girl's free hand. Something about this explained the meaning of words within Helen, and Anne could immediately see in her face that she finally understood.

Helen immediately asked Anne for the name of the pump to be spelled on her hand and then the name of the trellis. All the way back to the house Helen learned the name of everything she touched and also asked for Anne's name. Anne spelled the name "Teacher" on Helen's hand. Within the next few hours Helen learned the spelling of 30 new words. It wasn't long before Anne was teaching Helen to read, first with raised letters and later with Braille, and then she learned to write with both ordinary and Braille typewriters.

On June 28, 1904, Helen graduated from Radcliffe College, becoming the first deaf and blind person to earn a Bachelor of Arts degree (what an achievement!). She dedicated her life to helping people with these disabilities.

By this time Helen had become famous. She continued to visit the famous inventor, Alexander Graham Bell, and visited President Cleveland at the White House.

Helen, and Anne Sullivan, filled the following years with lecture tours, speaking of her experiences and beliefs to enthralled crowds. Her talks were interpreted sentence by sentence by Anne, and were followed by question and answer sessions.

Helen then took to vaudeville. The vaudeville appearances continued with Helen answering a wide range of questions about her life and her politics and Anne translating Helen's answers for the audience. They were earning up to $2,000 a week, a considerable sum of money at the time.

In the early 1930s Anne's health deteriorated and in 1936 she passed away. When Anne died, Polly Thomson took Anne's place. Helen and Polly moved to Connecticut, which would be Helen's home for the rest of her life.

After World War II, Helen and Polly spent years traveling the world fund-raising for the American Foundation for the Overseas Blind. They visited Japan, Australia, South America, Europe, and Africa.

In 1957 Polly had a stroke and died on March 21, 1960. The nurse who had been brought in to care for Polly in her last years, Winnie Corbally, took care of Helen in her remaining years.

In October 1961 Helen suffered the first of a series of strokes, and her public life drew to a close. Her last years were not, however, without excitement. In 1964 Helen was awarded by President Lyndon Johnson, the Presidential Medal of Freedom, the nation's highest civilian award. A year later she was elected to the Women's Hall of Fame at the New York World's Fair.

On June 1, 1968, at Arcan Ridge, Helen Keller died peacefully in her sleep.

Helen's dedication, courage, and determination were based on her Christian faith and were recognized by all who knew her. Blindness could not knock her out. She altered our perception of the disabled and remapped the boundaries of sight and sense.

Helen was determined that she would not be limited by any disability but she would rise above weaknesses and change the lives of others who would follow after her. She was determined that no person would look on the disabled and consider them less in value. In Helen's own words:

"The public must learn that the blind man is neither genius nor a freak nor an idiot. He has a mind that can be educated, a hand which can be trained, ambitions which it is right for him to strive to realize, and it is the duty of the public to help him make the best of himself so that he can win light through work."[7]

FAILURE IS NOT FINAL!

In the Irish uprising of 1848, men were captured, tried, and convicted of treason against Her

Majesty, Queen Victoria. All were sentenced to death...Passionate protest from all over the world persuaded the Queen to commute the death sentences.

The men were banished to Australia—as remote and full of prisoners as Russian Siberia. Years passed. In 1874 Queen Victoria learned that a Sir Charles Duffy who had been elected Prime Minister of Australia was the same Charles Duffy who had been banished 26 years earlier. She asked what had become of the other eight convicts. She learned that:

Patrick Donahue became a Brigadier General in the United States Army.
Morris Lyene became Attorney General for Australia.
Michael Ireland succeeded Lyene as Attorney General.
Thomas McGee became Minister of Agriculture for Canada.
Terrence McManus became a Brigadier General in the United States Army.
Thomas Meagher was elected Governor of Montana.
John Mitchell became a prominent New York politician and his son, John Purroy Mitchell, Mayor of New York City.
Richard O'Gorman became Governor of Newfoundland.

Big companies that declared bankruptcy before reaching success:

Quaker Oats (3 times)
Pepsi-Cola (3 times)
Borden's
Wrigley's (3 times)

Alexander Graham Bell, the inventor of the telephone, an invention without which the business world of today could not even begin to function, was hard-pressed to find a major backer. In 1876, the year he patented the telephone, Bell approached Western Union, then the largest communications company in America, and offered it exclusive rights to the invention for $100,000. William Orton, Western Union's president, turned down the offer, posing one of the most shortsighted questions in business history: "What use could this company make of an electrical toy?"

Thomas A. Edison knew 1,800 ways *not* to build a light bulb. As America's most prolific inventor, he was granted 1,093 patents by the U.S. Patent office, more than anyone else. His "inventions" included furniture made of cement and a way of using goldenrod for rubber.

Henry Ford failed and went broke five times before he finally succeeded. He forgot to put a reverse gear in the first car he manufactured. Then in 1957, he bragged about the car of the decade—the

Edsel, renowned for doors that wouldn't close, a hood that wouldn't open, paint that peeled, a horn that stuck, and a reputation that made it impossible to resell. However, Ford's future track record contains years of success stories.

Charles Schulz, the cartoonist who drew "Peanuts," was told by his high school's yearbook staff that his cartoons were not acceptable for the annual. But Schulz knew that he was of importance to God. He kept on drawing and eventually became known internationally for his considerable talent.

Daniel Defoe took *Robinson Crusoe* to 20 publishers before it was finally published. The book has been a best-seller for over 250 years and has been translated into ten languages.

ENDNOTES

1. http://justus.anglican.org/resources/bio/74.html

2. http://www.laza.org/eng/strength.htm

3. http://chi.gospelcom.net/dailyf/2001/01/daily-01-08-2001.shtml

4. http://www.post-gazette.com/pg/06008/633940.stm

5. http://www.rnib.org.uk/xpedio/groups/public/documents/publicwebsite/public_keller.hcsp

6. http://www.time.com/time/time100/
   heroes/profile/keller01.html
7. http://www.rnib.org.uk/xpedio/groups/
   public/documents/publicwebsite/
   public_keller.hcsp

Chapter 9

"SOMETHING GREAT IS ABOUT TO HAPPEN!"

(A WORD FROM CHANCELLOR ORAL ROBERTS)

T HE following is a letter that I received from Chancellor Oral Roberts after he saw me get punched in the eye at the altar on Sunday, November 20, 2005. Let this word minister to you as you read it.

November 23, 2005
Pastor Billy Joe Daugherty
Victory Christian Center
Tulsa, Oklahoma

My dear Pastor Billy Joe, Sharon, and all of you dear saints of Victory Christian Center:

Just this past week while in my home here in Southern California, we watched the scene on television where after Billy Joe had completed his sermon and was having an altar call with the unsaved, a man slugged him and brought cuts to his face with the blood streaming down.

I know that it must have been a shocking moment! But it took me back to July 1947 when I first came to Tulsa and had my first healing crusade on North Main in Pastor Steve Pringle's big tent seating 1,000. One night while the place was jammed out with the sick and hurting, I was up on the platform preaching the healing power of God for our generation. A man became angry and came to the back of the tent, pulled out a gun, aimed it at my head, and pulled the trigger. The bullet plowed a few inches above my head. There was a loud pop, but not knowing what it was, I kept on preaching the gospel. The next morning when we awakened and looked at our Tulsa newspaper, we saw the headlines, "Oral Roberts, Young Healing Evangelist, Shot At in Big Tent."

In a matter of hours an unknown young preacher who had just started out to obey God's call on his life and take His healing power to his generation was headline news across America. And I was known almost instantly at a time when virtually nobody knew about me.

Pastors from all over the country read about it and many of them flew to Tulsa to see what was going on. They began to call me to come to their churches to preach and pray for the sick.

That man was arrested and we went down the next day where he was in jail and I asked him why he tried to kill me. He said something came over him and told him to get me out of the way.

I realized it was the devil trying to kill me and to stop the beginning of the healing ministry that has touched the entire world and the building of Oral Roberts University. Out of ORU came two young people, Billy Joe and Sharon Daugherty, graduating with their degrees, but above all getting into the miracle power of God for their lives and beginning Victory Christian Center. Because they could not find a building large enough for their ever-increasing crowds, I suggested to Billy Joe that he consider Mabee Center. He came and you dear people have risen up, responding to his anointed ministry of the miracle power of God. You have come by the thousands, and Mabee Center has been sanctified with the gospel of signs and wonders by the ministry of Billy Joe and Sharon Daugherty. His ministry has spread throughout the world including building schools and churches in [many] nations. Victory Christian Center has become the largest church in Tulsa and out of it came Victory School which is impacting thousands of young people, many of whom have gone on to Oral Roberts University, including several of my own grandchildren. And now a new sanctuary is being built across the street from Mabee Center. The ministries have remained in close fellowship and in the miracle-working power of God.

It is no wonder to me that the devil would like to kill the messenger. He would like to take out 'the man of God.' He would like to stop the spread of the miracle of Seed-Faith that you have embraced with all your heart and your ministry of giving and receiving.

But thank God, Billy Joe only got some cuts and a bloody face. There was no way to stop him. He simply went back into the pulpit and continued to preach the gospel of Jesus Christ with love and a forgiving spirit.

What I feel in my spirit as the tears come to my eyes and the anointing of God flows through my being is that 'Something great is about to happen!' Victory Christian Center and its outreaches are about to impact Tulsa and the world in a new and more powerful way. You are about to feel an invasion of God's Holy Spirit in your life. I can feel it now! I feel like I am with you, this Sunday after the man's attack, standing beside Pastor Billy Joe and Sharon.

I love you! I prayed for you today! And with my family, Richard and Lindsay, and dear Evelyn who went to heaven last May 4, we are standing with you in every way. We believe that the best is yet to come.

I am now lifting my hands to Jesus and am ready to give a shout of praise to the Lord. Will you join me now as I shout praise to God? Now, everybody! Amen and Amen!

I am sending my seed of faith of $1,000 as my vote of victory coming out of this altercation from a man who obviously did not know what he was doing or was under the influence of something negative. God is going to help you finish the new sanctuary. He is going to enlarge your borders like He enlarged the coast of Jabez in 1 Chronicles. He is going to bless your enlarged borders and keep His hand on your life that no evil will overcome you.

I send this seed of faith out of my own need, knowing that God will supply my needs abundantly.

With all my love and my prayers,

Oral Roberts

Oral Roberts

My word to you is, if something bad happens and you get hit during your journey through life, believe that something great is going to happen and that God will turn it around!

JESUS WANTS YOU HEALED AND WHOLE

After the altar punch, God said to me, "This deal is not about you. *It's about My Son Jesus healing the hurts of suffering people."* God wants to get His message out that He is the Healer of broken hearts and that you can forgive and get up.

Jesus is going to help you regardless of the hit you took, the violation of your body, the rejection, the court proceeding, or whatever the situation. Jesus sees the entire situation, the things that the devil meant for evil, and as you praise on through, He will turn the evil for your good. It will be a story for His glory!

For every assignment against the righteous, we say, "What You have done, Lord, cancels the work of the enemy. Your resurrection overcomes death. Your joy overcomes sorrow. Your victory overcomes our defeats, and Your success triumphs over our failures in the name of Jesus."

There is nothing that has happened to you that is worse than what happened to Jesus. You could say to me, "Pastor, you don't know what I've been through." That's true, but I do know what Jesus went through and it is greater than anything any of us have ever been hit with. He went through it, He forgave, He was raised up, and He went on with what His Father called Him to do. Jesus said, *"As the Father has sent Me, I also send you...Receive the Holy Spirit"* (John 20:21-22).

You need to say: Jesus, help me every day to forgive and release those who have hurt or offended me. Help me to let go of the past and rise up into victory in all of the assignments You have called me to do.

PERSONAL PRAYER OF COMMITMENT

IF you are in the pigpen like the prodigal son, or you have failed and you are living in regret over the past, it's time to say "yes" to Jesus Christ. It's time to come to your senses and realize that there is an emptiness on the inside and a lack of fulfillment in your life without Christ.

When many people are confronted with the opportunity to accept Jesus Christ, they say, "I'm not ready." There's not a thing you can do to get ready, except to be willing to accept Him. You can't turn over a new leaf and suddenly get right with God. You can't patch up a lot of things and suddenly get ready. You can't cleanse yourself and then accept Jesus. You can only come to God just as you are!

You may need to admit, like the prodigal son, "I've got to go back to Father's house just the way I am. I'm broke, empty, and hurting." The Father will receive you. He's waiting with open arms to receive you. He'll heal your hurts and cleanse you from sin. Your turning to God is the power of repentance that God uses to work in your life. Just open your heart and say, Lord, cleanse me. Renew me. Give me a new start. I need to start over.

If you have grown up knowing about the Lord, but you've never entered a personal relationship with Him, it's your day to start over. If it has been a game for you to go to church and say the right things to your family, but in your heart you really don't know Jesus, you can answer the high calling of God today by coming into a personal relationship with Jesus Christ.

Or if you are 80 years old and you've never accepted Jesus Christ as your Lord and Savior, it's not too late as long as you have breath! Today is your day to respond to Jesus. It's your day to start over.

If you're lukewarm in your belief, it's time to start over. The Spirit of God said through John:

"I know your works, that you are neither cold nor hot. I could wish you were cold or hot.

"So then, because you are lukewarm, and neither cold nor hot, I will vomit you out of My mouth. Because you say, 'I am rich, have become wealthy, and have need of nothing'—and do not know that you are wretched, miserable, poor, blind, and naked—I counsel you to buy from Me gold refined in the fire, that you may be rich; and white garments, that you may be clothed, that the shame of your nakedness may not be revealed; and anoint your eyes with eye salve, that you may see. As many as I love, I rebuke and chasten. Therefore be zealous and repent. Behold, I stand at the door and knock. If anyone hears My voice and opens the door, I will come in to him and dine with him, and he with Me" (Revelation 3:15-20).

It's time to wake up, to shake off the lukewarmness and the lethargy, and become hot for God! Regardless of what your past has been, today is your day to rise above the hits you have taken and start over!

To accept Jesus Christ as your personal Savior and Lord, pray with me right now:

Father, I come to You now in the name of Jesus. I've been hit and I feel like I'm down for the count. I need Your help to get up and to get on the path You have ordained for me.

I acknowledge that Jesus Christ is Your Son, and I believe in my heart that He gave His blood on Calvary to pay for my sin, poverty, sickness, and spiritual death so I can live life to the fullest and complete Your assignment for me.

I renounce every work of darkness, and I confess You now, Jesus, as my personal Savior and Lord.

Thank You for empowering me with Your Spirit, Lord, so I can be a bold witness of You and Your kind of life and love in my area of influence.

Help me to be quick to forgive and release those who are responsible for the hits that have come in my life. Bless them, Lord, and transform them into Your image and likeness. Lead them in the way You would have them go, Lord.

Thank You for healing me, making me whole, and strengthening me, Lord, for my new life in You! Today is a new day for me!

_____

(Signature)

_____

(Date)

FOR OTHER BOOKS BY THE AUTHOR,

contact
www.victory.com
or
call 918-491-7700.

Or write to:

Victory Christian Center
7700 South Lewis Avenue
Tulsa, OK 74136-7700

Additional copies of this book and other book titles from DESTINY IMAGE are available at your local bookstore.

Call toll free: 1-800-722-6774.

Send a request for a catalog to:

Destiny Image® Publishers, Inc.

P.O. Box 310

Shippensburg, PA 17257-0310

"Speaking to the Purposes of God for This Generation and for the Generations to Come"

For a complete list of our titles, visit us at www.destinyimage.com